Classics
ST HELENS
RUGBY LEAGUE FOOTBALL CLUB

Make mine a treble! Saints' players on their open-topped bus celebrate the team's Grand Final success of 2000, together with the World Club Championship and Challenge Cup triumphs of 2001 – a fantastic record of achievement! From left to right: Anthony Sullivan, skipper Chris Joynt, Kevin Iro, Mark Edmonson, Sonny Nickle, John Stankevitch and Keiron Cunningham. We are truly in an era of classic matches – long may they continue!

Classics
ST HELENS
RUGBY LEAGUE FOOTBALL CLUB

ALEX SERVICE & DENIS WHITTLE

TEMPUS

Acknowledgements

The authors would like to thank the following people and organisations for their help in making this publication possible. St Helens Library gave us the opportunity to review match details sometimes lost in the mists of time from the files of the *St Helens Reporter* and *Newspaper and Advertiser. The Rugby Leaguer* – alas no longer in its original guise – was a rich source of information, and we would like to thank John Riding, Bernard Platt, Brian Peers, Geoff Pimblett, Sig Kasatkin and Gerald Webster for some excellent photographic contributions. Robert Gate, the doyen of Rugby League historians, has given us much help and inspiration over the years, together with the members of the Saints' Heritage Society, who have provided much encouragement and support. A special mention must go to Simon Dawson, Head of Marketing and Media at Knowsley Road, for his assistance. James Howarth at Tempus has also been of great help to us in putting this publication together. Special thanks to Paul Sculthorpe for the foreword – he is well on the way towards establishing himself as one of Rugby League's all-time greats! Last, but by no means least, to the players, officials and supporters of the team renowned as the great entertainers of the thirteen-a-side code. Long live the Saints.

First published 2002

Tempus Publishing Limited
The Mill, Brimscombe Port,
Stroud, Gloucestershire, GL5 2QG

© Alex Service and Denis Whittle, 2002

The right of Alex Service and Denis Whittle to be identified as the Authors of this work has been asserted by them in accordance with the Copyrights, Designs and Patents Act 1988.

All rights reserved. No part of this book may be reprinted or reproduced or utilised in any form or by any electronic, mechanical or other means, now known or hereafter invented, including photocopying and recording, or in any information storage or retrieval system, without the permission in writing from the Publishers.

British Library Cataloguing in Publication Data.
A catalogue record for this book is available from the British Library.

ISBN 0 7524 2706 7

Typesetting and origination by Tempus Publishing Limited
Printed in Great Britain by Midway Colour Print, Wiltshire

Introduction

The purpose of this book is two-fold. First of all, it has always been a desire for both of us to commemorate some of the finest matches in the Saints' long and eventful history and this task has given us the greatest of pleasure! We have tried to cover matches right across the historical spectrum, from the early days of the Northern Union to the Super League. Yet we realise that our choices may well create controversy and discussion. Quite right too! The second purpose is therefore to stimulate debate and to make Saints' fans think of their own favourite clashes. Let's face it...we all have our own particularly special matches – for a whole variety of reasons! Indeed, a look at the authors' 'best five' reveals both uniformity and diversity in their choice of classic matches seen:

Alex Service's 'Choice Cuts'

Saints v. Halifax (Championship final 1966)
Saints v. Wigan (Championship final 1971)
Saints v. Widnes (Challenge Cup final 1976)
Saints v. Bradford Bulls (Challenge Cup final 1996)
Saints v. Brisbane Broncos (World Club Challenge 2001)

Denis Whittle's 'Pick of the Crop'

Saints v. Huddersfield (Championship Play-Off 1953)
Saints v. Halifax (Challenge Cup final (Challenge Cup final 1956)
Saints v. New Zealand (Tour Match 1989)
Saints v. Bradford Bulls (Challenge Cup final 1996)
Saints v. Brisbane Broncos (World Club Challenge 2001)

Bubbling under? What about the fantastic elimination play-off match against Bradford Bulls at Knowsley Road in 2001? The chances are that we will never see such a fantastic finish again! The match we would most have liked to see? The Lancashire Cup final of 1926, billed as the Championship of St Helens, between the Saints and the Recs. What an occasion that must have been!

Enjoy your rugby league!

Alex Service
Denis Whittle

The 50 Classic Matches

1896/97	St Helens v. Batley	Challenge Cup final	8
1897/98	St Helens v. Oldham	League Match	10
1907/08	St Helens v. New Zealand	Tour Match	12
1914/15	St Helens v. Rochdale Hornets	Challenge Cup semi-final	14
1926/27	St Helens v. St Helens Recs	Lancashire Cup final	16
1929/30	St Helens v. Australia	Tour Match	18
1929/30	St Helens v. Wigan	Challenge Cup semi-final	20
1931/32	St Helens v. Huddersfield	Championship final	22
1944/45	St Helens v. Wigan	League Match	24
1946/47	Wigan v. St Helens	League Match	26
1952/53	St Helens v. Huddersfield	Championship play-off	28
1953/54	St Helens v. Wigan	Lancashire Cup final	30
1955/56	St Helens v. Barrow	Challenge Cup semi-final	32
1955/56	St Helens v. Halifax	Challenge Cup final	34
1956/57	St Helens v. Australia	Tour Match	38
1957/58	St Helens v. Leeds	League Match	40
1958/59	St Helens v. Hunslet	Championship final	42
1960/61	St Helens v. Hull	Challenge Cup semi-final	46
1960/61	St Helens v. Wigan	Challenge Cup semi-final	48
1964/65	St Helens v. Warrington	League Match	52
1965/66	St Helens v. Hull KR	Championship play-off	54
1965/66	St Helens v. Wigan	Challenge Cup final	56
1965/66	St Helens v. Halifax	Championship final	60
1969/70	St Helens v. Leeds	Championship final	62
1970/71	Wigan v. St Helens	Floodlit Trophy semi-final	64
1970/71	St Helens v. Wigan	Championship final	66
1971/72	St Helens v. Leeds	Challenge Cup final	68
1975/76	St Helens v. Widnes	Challenge Cup final	72
1977/78	St Helens v. Leeds	Challenge Cup final	76
1984/85	Wigan v. St Helens	Lancashire Cup final	78
1984/85	St Helens v. Hull KR	Premiership final	80
1986/87	St Helens v. Halifax	Challenge Cup final	84
1987/88	Wigan v. St Helens	League Match	86
1987/88	St Helens v. Leeds	John Player Trophy final	88
1987/88	Warrington v. St Helens	Challenge Cup	90
1988/89	St Helens v. Widnes	Challenge Cup semi-final	92
1989/90	St Helens v. New Zealand	Tour Match	94
1990/91	St Helens v. Widnes	Challenge Cup semi-final	96
1991/92	St Helens v. Wigan	Lancashire Cup semi-final	98
1991/92	Leeds v. St Helens	Challenge Cup	100
1992/93	St Helens v. Wigan	League Match	104
1992/93	St Helens v. Wigan	Premiership final	106

1993/94	St Helens v. Bradford Northern	League Match	108
1996	St Helens v. Bradford Bulls	Challenge Cup final	110
1996	London Broncos v. St Helens	League Match	114
1997	St Helens v. Salford	Challenge Cup semi-final	116
1999	St Helens v. Bradford Bulls	Grand Final	118
2000	St Helens v. Bradford Bulls	Qualifying play-off	120
2000	St Helens v. Wigan	Grand Final	122
2001	St Helens v. Brisbane Broncos	World Club Challenge	126

Foreword

What a last two years it has been – many highs and not many lows! Firstly, winning the 1999 Grand Final against Bradford Bulls. Personally, that game stands out, as it was my first-ever final and it was an incredible feeling to win it. Then, to do it all again in 2000 was an outstanding achievement, especially against the Old Enemy, Wigan! On the road to that final, who will ever forget the match against Bradford at Knowsley Road and that try of Joynty's! It was a game we truly deserved to win, but we left it to the last ten seconds and did it in true Saints' style!

The win against Wigan gave us the chance again to test ourselves against the best in the world – the Brisbane Broncos – and what a win it was! To be crowned World Club Champions was very special to the players, the club and the fans, who very much contributed to our success. Then, all thoughts were on winning the Challenge Cup. The performance against Bradford in the final was a ruthless one. It wasn't a pretty game, but keeping them try-less was an indication of how well we played – with even the Bradford players saying they could have played for another week and still not scored! The 'treble' was ours!

The end of 2001 saw some great servants to Saints move on. Anthony Sullivan moved to Welsh rugby union after seeing out his testimonial year. The 'Beast', Kevin Iro, decided to hang up his boots after a glittering career and probably one of the best overseas signings to this country – David Fairleigh – retired back to Australia. With the younger members of the squad establishing themselves as top players in Super League, there looks to be many more good times ahead for the Saints. Roll on those trophies…!

Paul Sculthorpe
St Helens and Great Britain
May 2002

St Helens v. Batley Challenge Cup final

24 April 1897
Headingley, Leeds

Attendance: 13,492
Referee: Mr Smith (Widnes)

It seems hard to believe that when the Rugby League Challenge Cup competition was first launched in 1897, Batley were the pride of the White Rose county and the overwhelming favourites to lift the trophy! The Saints were unlikely finalists, showing indifferent form in the League. Yet the team really pulled out the stops in the Cup, defeating Lees, Wigan, Tyldesley and Swinton on their way to the Headingley showdown. The St Helens team and officials caught the ten past nine train to Leeds, arriving at noon, where they were taken to Headingley by horse-drawn carriage!

In front of an expectant crowd, the St Helens captain, Tom Foulkes, the grandfather of Manchester United centre half Bill, won the toss and decided to take advantage of the strong breeze. Yet the Batley forwards began to dominate and soon the first-ever points were scored – a drop-goal in fact – by Batley stand off Oakland. Yorkshire's Gallant Youths extended their lead shortly afterwards. Who says the cross-kick is a modern Bobbie Goulding invention? Winger Wattie Davies did just that for his captain John Goodall, who caught the ball and cantered over the line. Saints' Tom Foulkes insisted he was off-side, but there were no television replays or video referees to back him up then!

Despite losing stand-off Little, with Briers leaving the pack to compensate, the Saints gave the 'Gallant Youths' a real fright in the third quarter. A sliced drop-goal from Goodall was fielded by Saints' Cumbrian winger 'Bob' Doherty, who shrugged off two attempted tackles. A dummy to the supporting Jacques, a quick turn and a lovely timed pass fizzed out to Dave Traynor on the right. The burly winger flew along the touchline, brushing aside three white-shirted tacklers, before touching down as close to the posts as he could. Unfortunately, the conversion was missed by scrum-half Jacques. Batley clinched a 10-3 success with a 'forward rush' try by Munns in the corner, so typical of the game in those days.

The Saints ruefully collected their runners-up medals and reflected on what might have been. David Traynor received special praise for his marvellous score. It was fully justified too, as it was the only time that the Batley line had been crossed during the competition! The Saints had at least played their part in creating a bit of history, even if their name would not be inscribed on the gleaming trophy for another 59 years.

From those early beginnings at Headingley, the Challenge Cup has grown into Rugby League's most famous knock-out competition, worth thousands of pounds to the winners. Receipts from that first final totalled just £624 and the players were smaller too. The average St Helens player in 1897, typified by forward William 'Kitty' Briers, would be 5ft 7in, and weigh 11st 11lb! The average height and weight of the Saints' team which played Leeds in the 1972 final is 13st 4lb, and 5ft 9in in height! Doubtless the Batley cup finalists would have faced a forward like John Mantle – 6ft 2in and 15st 4lb – with great respect and more than a little trepidation!

Half time: 0-7

St Helens 3
Try: Traynor

Batley 10
Tries: Goodall, Munns
Drop goal: Oakland

St Helens v. Batley

Right: David Traynor, Saints' Widnes-born winger, who scored the club's first ever try in a Challenge Cup final, pictured in his Lancashire jersey and cap.

Below: Saints forward John Mantle powers over the Wigan line during the 1966 Challenge Cup final. The Batley team of 1897 would certainly have treated him with the utmost respect!

St Helens: T. Foulkes (*captain*); R. Doherty, D. Traynor, J. Barnes, R. O'Hara; F. Little, W. Jacques; T. Winstanley, W. Briers, W. Winstanley, T. Reynolds, J. Thompson, P. Dale, S. Rimmer, W. Whiteley.

Batley: A. Garner; W. Davies, D. Fitzgerald, J. Goodall (*captain*), J. Shaw; J. Oakland, H. Goodall; M. Shackleton, J. Gath, G. Maine, R. Spurr, F. Fisher, C. Stubley, J. Littlewood, J. Munns.

St Helens v. Oldham Lancashire Senior Competition

1 October 1898
Knowsley Road, St Helens

Attendance: 4,000
Referee: Mr Dillon (Warrington)

Thatto Heath has always been a fertile breeding ground for rugby league talent. In the formative years of the Northern Union, two players from this famous district of St Helens starred for the Saints – Tom Foulkes, a solid, reliable full-back and William 'Kitty' Briers, a tremendously mobile forward, who had a habit of scoring vital tries when the need arose. When the Roughyeds from Oldham came to Knowsley Road in the autumn of 1898, they did so as one of the most powerful teams in the game – champions of the Lancashire Senior Competition – and were ready to beat their West Lancashire neighbours out of sight!

It was so different in those early days after the famous 'split', with the legacy of eight forwards in a fifteen-a-side game, resulting in an abundance of mauls and forward rushes. William Briers was an expert dribbler with a rugby ball and once scored a try against Broughton by controlling the leather for virtually the length of the field before diving over to secure the points. Although never a really big man, weighing just thirteen stones, he had tremendous shoulder muscles, honed daily as a blacksmith's striker at nearby Lea Green Colliery. He was no slouch either, running 100 yards in twelve seconds.

For the Oldham match, Briers played at half-back, where it was hoped his undoubted strength and mobility would unsettle the visitors. Perhaps it was over-confidence on the part of Oldham. At the end of the game, the scintillating Saints had chalked up one of their most famous victories to the tune of 15-9. It was a superb team performance and a personal triumph for Kitty Briers, who scored a hat-trick of tries, all three coming in a blistering first half in which the Saints also kept a clean sheet. Try number one came when Thomas, the Oldham winger, had a clearance kick charged down in his own twenty-five. Although full-back Woodhead re-gathered, he was promptly clattered by Saints' second-rower Joe Thompson and the ball came loose. It was Briers who swooped to ground the ball for the all-important opener. Woodhead again failed to find touch shortly after and the home forwards stormed menacingly towards the Oldham line, ending when Briers threw himself headlong to touch down. Cumbrian front-rower Bill Whiteley and local lad Peter Dale led another rush into enemy territory. It seemed inevitable that Kitty Briers would once again be on hand to complete matters! Three goals from David Traynor ensured a healthy 15-0 half-time lead and much needed it was too. Oldham were shaken from their lethargy after the break and produced more like their true form, with wingers Thomas and Rees scoring three tries between them. But it was too little too late!

To their undoubted credit, a somewhat stunned Oldham side accepted defeat like true gentlemen. Before the match at the Watersheddings later in the season, they presented Kitty Briers with a special cap to mark his hat-trick, before exacting due revenge against St Helens with a 16-0 success!

Kitty Briers, so named because he was kitty-pawed, or left-handed, was a model of consistency who went on to make 515 appearances for the Saints; this astonishing statistic does not include the matches he played in the pre-Northern Union days. He proved his mobility by scoring 116 tries for his club, a huge total for someone who played the bulk of his rugby as a forward. But none were more memorable than the three which helped to defeat the mighty Roughyeds at Knowsley Road in 1898!

Half time: 15-0

St Helens 15
 Tries: Briers (3)
 Goals: Traynor (3)

Oldham 9
 Tries: Williams (2), Thomas

St Helens v. Oldham

St Helens RLFC, 1907/08. Ten years on and Kitty Briers is still a fixture in the forward pack! The team are photographed in the yard of their club headquarters, the Talbot Hotel in Duke Street, where Saints and their opponents would get changed before riding on an open wagonnette to Knowsley Road. Club colours? Various hooped combinations of red, amber and black. From left to right, back row: Smith (trainer), J. Appleton (assistant trainer), T. Phillips (chairman), J. Bradburn, J. Pope, F. Lee, J. Manchester, J. Whiston. Middle row: J. Atkinson, J. Mavity, W. Hillen, J. Creevey (captain), C. Creevey, F. Mooney. Front row: W. Briers, E. Toole, M. Creevey.

St Helens: T. Foulkes (*captain*); R. Doherty, J. Barnes, D. Traynor, Siddall; W. Briers, Boyle; P. Dale, W. Whiteley, J. Simpson, T. Reynolds, Stubbings, W. Winstanley, J. Thompson, J. Chapman.

Oldham: F. Woodhead; R. Thomas, T. Davies, S. Lees (*captain*), S. Williams; J. Lawton, M. Rees; E. Bonser, G. Frater, R. Porter, F. Davies, J. Lees, R. Edwards, J. Merrill, H. Broome.

St Helens v. New Zealand Tour Match

22 February 1908
Knowsley Road, St Helens

Attendance: 3,000
Referee: Mr Priestley (Salford)

It was in the 1907/08 season that the newly-formed professional New Zealand international team visited Britain for the first time. They were managed by a twenty-four-year-old post office clerk from Wellington, Albert Henry Baskerville who had no previous experience of rugby in the Northern Union. The tour caused uproar in New Zealand, where professionalism was a dirty word. In London, their Agent General expressed the opinion that the 'All Golds', as they were called, would bring no credit to their country. Despite the lack of official support and their inexperience of the new code, the tour was an outstanding success overall. The long-awaited visit to Knowsley Road took place on 13 October 1907, where the Kiwis, with their Australian guest three-quarter Herbert 'Dally' Messenger in dazzling form, beat the Saints 24-5. Clad in their narrow-rimmed straw hats emblazoned with the silvery fern, the Colonials were a popular side both on and off the field. The St Helens public took them to their hearts. It was very much a mutual attraction, as the New Zealanders felt more at home in the 'Pill and Glass' town than anywhere else on tour. There was certainly a strong link with their own country, as Richard Seddon, the popular New Zealand prime minister from 1893 to 1906 was born in St Helens. During their stay, the players made a pilgrimage to his birthplace and were photographed outside the cottage half-way up Eccleston Hill, which stands to this day!

The All Blacks enjoyed themselves so much that they returned in the New Year to play a second match at Knowsley Road and revisited the many friends they had made in the town. By a strange coincidence, the return fixture, just like the first, was a washout weather-wise. Strong winds and heavy rain kept the attendance down to 3,000, yet it proved to be a marvellous spectacle of fast, open football for the faithful few. Appearing for the first time on tour was Albert Baskerville, who was no mean player in his own right! Only his secretarial duties prevented him from playing in more matches.

'Dickie' Wynyard kicked off for the visitors against the gale and it was not long before the home side took full advantage. Lightning-fast winger Jack Manchester scored after a forward rush, as New Zealand full-back 'Jum' Turtill hesitated before attempting to kick the ball dead. Saints kept up the pressure and play was restricted to the All Blacks' quarter of the field. After further forward pressure, Frank 'Boyler' Lee picked up a loose ball and dashed over the line. Jimmy Creevey added a neat conversion. Immediately afterwards, the same player made a tactical left-foot drop across the field towards Manchester. To everyone's surprise and delight the wind completely turned the course of the ball and carried it between the posts!

Unfortunately, Saints' ten-point advantage did not last too long after the interval. 'Maori' Tyler opened the visitors' account with a brilliant solo touchdown. Shortly after, scrum-half Wynyard scored two virtually identical tries from the base of the scrum. 'Dally' Messenger converted the second to give the All Blacks the lead. Towards the end of the game, there were great cheers as Baskerville expertly collected a cross-kick and crashed over near the posts. Messenger duly converted. It was to be a fine epitaph for 'Baski,' who tragically was to die of pneumonia in Australia on the last leg of the tour. 'Massa' Johnson completed the scoring to set the scene on a delightful exhibition of rugby.

Half time: 10-0

St Helens 10
Tries: Lee, Manchester
Goals: J. Creevey (2)

New Zealand 21
Tries: R. Wynyard (2), Tyler, Johnson, Baskerville
Goals: Messenger (3)

St Helens v. New Zealand

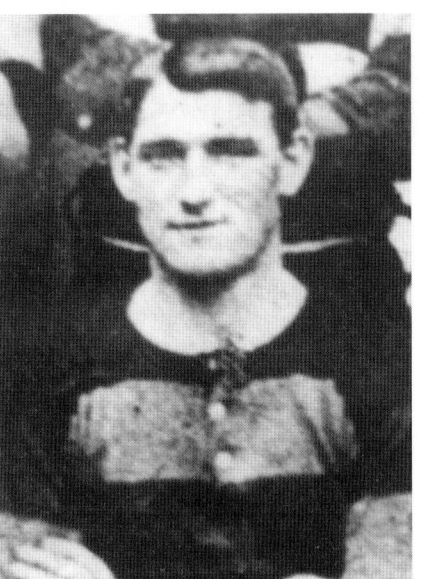

Right: Centre Jimmy Creevey, Saints' captain against the All Blacks, who kicked two goals in the match, featured in the red, amber and black hooped jerseys in vogue at the time.

Below: Two members of the pioneering All Blacks signed for St Helens. Scrum-half Arthur Kelly was the first, followed by star full-back Hubert Sydney 'Jum' Turtill, who became a firm favourite with the Knowsley Road faithful.

THE NEW ZEALAND TEAM.
R. Wynward. A. Lile. D. Gilchrist. E. Tyne. C. Dunning. W. Tyler.
A.H.Baskerville C.J.Pearce. A.F.Kelly. J.A.Lavery. D.G.Fraser. A.Callam. C.A.Byrne. W.T.Wynyard. J.H.Smith.
(Sec. and Promoter). [Hodgson *(Non-player)*. H.S.Turtill.
W.Johnston. William Trevarthen. H H.Messenger. C.E.Wrigley. G.W.Smith. H.R.Wright. D.M'Gregor. W.Mackrell.
[Harold Rowe. L. B. Todd. T. Cross.

St Helens: J. Atkinson; J. Creevey (*captain*), J. Evans, W. Hillen, J. Manchester; M. Creevey, F. Trenwith; W. Briers, F. Lee, J. Pope, Holmes, W. Wharton, J. Mavitty.

New Zealand: H. Turtill; H. Messenger, H. Rowe, E. Tyne, E. Wrigley, W. Tyler; R. Wynyard, H. Wright (*captain*), W. Johnson, C. Pearce, A. Baskerville, C. Dunning, W. Trevarthen.

St Helens v. Rochdale Hornets Challenge Cup semi-final

24 April 1915
Central Park, Wigan

Attendance: 10,000
Referee: Mr Renton (Hunslet)

By the start of the 1914/15 season, Britain had entered the war against Germany. The Northern Union decided to allow recruiting on grounds and to regard the game as a form of wartime entertainment for the forces and workers at home. St Helens suffered like most clubs, with players and spectators joining the forces and others taking up vital Home Front jobs.

Yet the St Helens club could still call upon players like the inspirational Tom Barton, a fast, rugged three-quarter, and tough little scrum-half Fred Trenwith from Cumbria. When the Challenge Cup came round, in the New Year, the Saints progressed to the semi-finals for the first time since 1897, winning every game away from Knowsley Road. They had a unique 'set-piece' move involving Trenwith, which had the code-name 'Beechams'. He would pick up from the scrum base and the forwards would open out like a fan, to allow him to burrow his way through towards the try-line! It so irritated the spectators at Keighley that they pelted the referee with all sorts of projectiles after Trenwith's winning try in the quarter-final. Their ground was closed for the rest of the season as a result!

The 'Human Torpedo' was at it again in the first semi-final, at Warrington, against the much-fancied Rochdale Hornets. His try could only earn a 5-5 draw, however, with Tom Barton booting over a penalty for good measure. The deadlock actually extended into half an hour's extra time! St Helens had upset the rhythm of the Rochdale side by adopting a 'punting and spoiling' game. These same tactics were used to good effect in the replay at Wigan three weeks later. Saints' full-back Roberts gave them a dream start with a superbly-taken drop-goal. Rochdale desperately tried to reduce the arrears, but were never allowed to get into their stride, courtesy of some solid tackling from the Saints' pack!

After the breakdown of yet another Hornets' attack, Tom White, the St Helens' centre, picked up the loose ball and hared away down the field. He shrugged off several would-be tacklers, sold an outrageous dummy to full-back English and streaked under the posts. Barton converted with ease and the Saints were well on their way to a marvellous 9-2 victory. When referee Frank Renton blew the final whistle, the cheers from players, committee and spectators were deafening! The victory certainly surprised many people within the game itself, a fact not lost on the rugby correspondent of the *St Helens Newspaper*: 'I wonder what would have been the fate of any prophet who foretold this year's events? If such a prophet had begun by declaring Germany would be fighting England in 1915, he might have been believed. If he had said Germany would be fighting England, France, Russia and a few more – he might have stood a chance of saving his skin, provided he could run. But if he had said that Saints would win every round of the cup up to the final, away from home – he would probably been extinguished as a dangerous lunatic at large!'

Lightning rarely strikes twice! Saints' game plan of playing the game in their opponents' half and tackling like demons had paid off, with one of the greatest results in the club's history. Unfortunately, in the final against Huddersfield's 'team of all the talents', seven days later, the Saints were well and truly thrashed 37-3. Mind you, there were ructions in the dressing room beforehand, when it was realised that the Saints would not be given a bonus for reaching the final. Tom Barton was the man who averted a players' strike in the minutes before the players were due out onto the pitch at Oldham – but that's another story.

Half time: 7-2

St Helens 9
Try: White
Goals: Barton (2)
Drop goal: Roberts

Rochdale Hornets 2
Drop goal: Jones

St Helens v. Rochdale Hornets

Right: Saints winger and captain Tom Barton, wearing his England cap. He was a key figure in the club's Challenge Cup run of 1914/15.

Below: St Helens versus Rochdale Hornets in the 1991 Lancashire Cup final. Saints' Australian star Phil Veivers scores one of his two tries in his team's 24-14 success.

St Helens: H. Roberts; T. Barton (*captain*), J. Flanagan, T. White, H. Greenall; F. Trenwith, M. Creevey; H. Heaton, S. Daniels, T. Durkin, G. Farrimond, W. Myers, W. Jackson.

Rochdale Hornets: M. English; Male, J. Corsi, G. Prudence (*captain*), J. Fairhurst; R. Schofield, E. Jones; W. Ashworth, J. Fitsimmonds, V. Slade, S. Carter, J. Bowers, W. Roman.

St Helens v. St Helens Recreation Lancashire Cup final

20 November 1926
Wilderspool Stadium, Warrington

Attendance: 19,430
Referee: Mr Horsfall (Batley)

This was the match the whole of St Helens wanted to see – The Saints against the Recs, their local rivals who had joined the professional ranks just after the First World War. The Recs were in their third final and looking for their second win in the competition. Saints desperately wanted to lift the trophy for the first time and grab some of the headlines away from their City Road neighbours. One thing was certain – the cup would end up somewhere in St Helens. Nearly 20,000 packed into Wilderspool, in driving rain. The unofficial championship of St Helens was about to be decided!

Shortly after kick-off, Tommy Dingsdale, the Recs' county full-back failed to find touch and a scrum was formed on his own twenty-five. Sparks flew immediately as the front rows greeted each other in customary fashion, resulting in a lecture from referee Horsfall. The scrum had hardly re-formed when the Recs pack were penalised. Saints' Welsh centre George Lewis made no mistake with the resultant goal kick and registered the first points after only a minute's play – a great start. A scramble ensued in the Saints' twenty-five and things looked dangerous when Groves was penalised for off-side. Unfortunately, Dingsdale fluffed the place kick and lost the chance of levelling the scores. It was a costly miss. After fifteen minutes, Alf Frodsham picked up the ball from some loose play and put in a tantalizing grubber kick which caught the Recs' defence flat-footed. Stand-off Les Fairclough, following up, picked up the ball cleverly on the bounce, beat Fildes with a beautiful swerve and shot under the posts for a superb opportunist try. Lewis converted with ease and the Saints were in the driving seat.

St Helens continued to enjoy most of the game and after 31 minutes, it was time for a piece of magic from wing-wizard Alf Ellaby. Receiving the ball from Lewis's well-timed pass, he put in a short kick over the head of his opposite number 'Durdock' Wilson. Full-back Dingsdale was caught out of position and Ellaby, more akin to the soccer code he left behind, dribbled over to score a splendid try in the corner, which was unconverted. As half time approached, the Recs made a desperate attempt to get back into the match. From a scrummage, Saints' loose forward Ernie Shaw was penalised for off-side. Jim Pyke took the kick at goal and reduced the lead by two points. Shortly afterwards, Mr Horsfall blew his whistle and half of Wilderspool cheered with delight.

The teams began the second half in rapidly deteriorating light. This time it was the turn of the Recs' pack to take the initiative. The Saints seemed quite content to stem their opponents' attacks and sit on their lead. Meanwhile, George Lewis got the Saints out of a tight corner with another splendid touch-finder. His skill and coolness were most valuable when the Recs threw everything into the assault on the Saints' line. Fifteen minutes to go – and no change in the score. The Saints' tackling was uncompromising and, by this time, the players were hardly distinguishable owing to several coats of mud and the gathering gloom. 'Tot' Wallace could be excused from giving a well-timed pass to a Saints' player by mistake in the circumstances! The last few minutes were characterized by a magnificent catch by Greenall in the failing light and an injury to Shaw, who forgot all about the pain when the final whistle blew! The cheering was deafening. Thousands jumped over the barriers intent on congratulating their mud-splattered heroes. Fairclough and Crooks were hoisted shoulder-high and carried through the sea of ecstatic St Helens spectators to the grandstand where the presentation was

Half time: 10-2

St Helens 10
Tries: Fairclough, Ellaby
Goals: Lewis (2)

St Helens Recreation 2
Goal: Pyke

St Helens v. St Helens Recreation

St Helens RLFC, Lancashire Cup Winners 1926/27. From left to right, back row: E. Smith (trainer), A. Horsfall (referee), L. Houghton, E. Shaw, F. Roffey (captain), R. Atkin, W. Clarey, N. Herbert (groundsman), C. Pennington (assistant trainer). Middle row: A. Ellaby, G. Lewis, C. Crooks, A. Frodsham, G. Cotton, A. Simm. Front row: L. Fairclough, B. Wilson (mascot), W. Groves.

to take place. Mr Rebbitt, the Lancashire county secretary, handed over the cup to Saints' skipper Fred Roffey amid thunderous applause. This was something special – the first major silverware won by the St Helens club. The Saints returned in triumph, first of all to the Town Hall, where a huge crowd had assembled outside to greet Roffey and his men. Then it was back to club headquarters at the White Lion Hotel in Church Street for a slap-up meal and a celebration drink or three! At the end of the evening, Ernie Shaw, still recovering from the blow on the head he received during the match, was determined to take the cup home with him to Runcorn! After a little gentle persuasion, however, Ernie handed it over to Saints chairman Jim May. That night, the glittering piece of silverware found a new home, albeit temporarily, under the chairman's bed!

St Helens: C. Crooks; G. Cotton, A. Frodsham, G. Lewis, A. Ellaby; L. Fairclough, W. Groves; R. Atkin, A. Simm, L. Houghton, W. Clarey, F. Roffey (*captain*), E. Shaw.

St Helens Recreation: T. Dingsdale; J. Wilson, A. Bailey, J. Pyke, J. Wallace; J. Greenall (*captain*), H. Halsall; Higgins, O. Dolan, G. Highcock, T. Smith, A. Fildes, W. Mulvanney.

St Helens v. Australia Tour Match

16 November 1929
Knowsley Road, St Helens

Attendance: 11,000
Referee: Mr Horsfall (Batley)

This superb encounter was, quite literally, a game of two halves, with Tom Gorman's fine Australian team dominating the first forty minutes and the Saints pack fighting back magnificently after half-time. To provide added spice, the home side incuded their three New Zealand signings, winger Roy Hardgrave, and forwards Lou Hutt and Trevor Hall. In the absence of star wing three-quarter Alf Ellaby, second-rower Ben Halfpenny was a surprise choice on the left flank. Yet the Widnes-born forward was no slouch and scored two crucial tries, as the Saints cut back the deficit to share the spoils at the final whistle – a truly classic encounter. Roy Hardgrave and skipper George Lewis were the other try-scorers for the home team, with the ever-reliable Lewis booting over three goals.

In the absence of Wakefield's Jonty Parkin, Saints stand-off Les Fairclough captained the Great Britain team in the First Test at Hull, which the home side lost heavily by 31-8. In the Second, at Headingley, Britain registered a 9-3 victory, minus Fairclough and with Alf Ellaby on the right wing. The final Test of the rubber, at Swinton, ended 0-0, the one and only time this has happened in the history of Rugby League Test Match football. As for the Saints in 1929/30, they gained a reputation as great entertainers, finishing on top of the table, despite a hectic fixture pile-up late in the campaign. Unfortunately, they lost out to Leeds in the Championship play-offs and were beaten by Widnes in the Challenge Cup final at Wembley – one of the great shocks in the history of the competition.

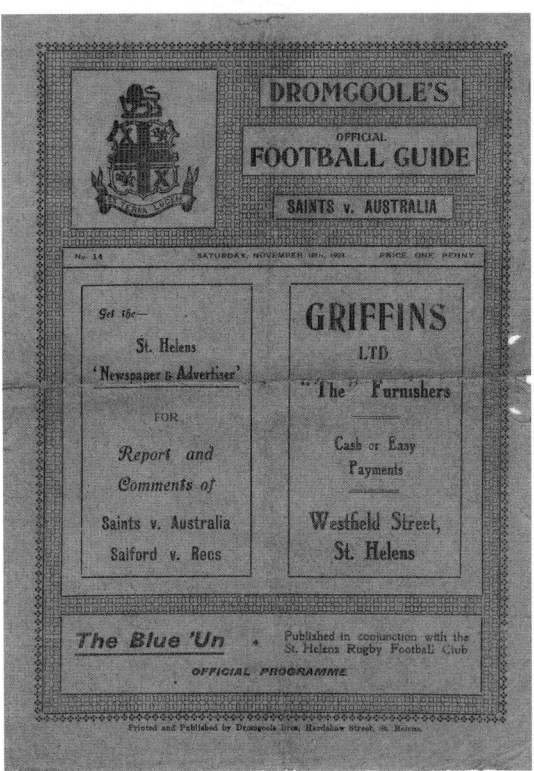

A rarity indeed! The programme for the match, called The Blue 'Un, was printed by local firm Dromgoole Brothers, a four-page broadsheet, printed in the same style for both Saints and St Helens Recreation matches. This particular issue contained a reference to a match against Castleford at Knowsley Road some three weeks previously, when Castleford centre Arthur Atkinson had kicked a 75-yard penalty goal, with the aid of a gale – the longest ever seen at the ground. The match ball had been signed and inscribed by the team and was presented to Atkinson himself at a later date.

Half time: 6-18

St Helens 18
Tries: Hardgrave (2), Halfpenny, Lewis
Goals: Lewis (3)

Australia 18
Tries: Finch (2), Kingston, Holmes
Goals: Finch (2), Laws

St Helens v. Australia

THE SAINTS BE PRAISED.

BERT WRIGHT'S CARICATURES AT THE ST. HELENS--AUSTRALIAN MATCH, WHICH WAS DRAWN, each side scoring eighteen points.

Bert Wright's cartoons were a regular feature of match reports in the *St Helens Newspaper* in the 1920s. He also used the soubriquet 'Saint Ellaby' after the famous St Helens winger Alf Ellaby. Copies of his cartoons could be bought separately from the newspaper offices and were popular with supporters at the time.

St Helens: C. Crooks; R. Hardgrave, G. Lewis (*captain*), W. Mercer, B. Halfpenny; L. Fairclough, E. Dowdall; L. Hutt, H. Unwin, L. Houghton, T. Hall, E. Hill, W. Groves.

Australia: F. Laws; H. Finch, P. Maher, T. Gorman (*captain*), J. Upton, J. Holmes, H. Kadwell, W. Brogan, A. Justice, E. Root, D. O'Dempsey, V. Armbruster, J. Kingston.

St Helens v. Wigan Challenge Cup semi-final

29 March 1930
Station Road, Swinton

Attendance: 37,169
Referee: Mr Robinson (Bradford)

Mouth-watering clashes between these deadly rivals are guaranteed terrace-packers and this one was no exception, as a crowd of 37,169 set a new record at Station Road. More than 6,000 Saints fans travelled by train from Shaw Street, Thatto Heath and St Helens Junction, while, with the East Lancashire Road not yet open, the route to Manchester was awash with rugby league traffic. With a first Wembley appearance for Saints and a second successive one in prospect for holders Wigan, the exchanges were predictably fast and furious, with no quarter asked or given and, on balance, a draw was perhaps a fair result.

Or was it? For both Saints' players and supporters were mystified by referee Robinson's penalty award to Wigan in the 60th minute, from which goal-kicking maestro Jim Sullivan gave his side a second bite of the Wembley cherry. From a selection angle, Saints took a calculated risk by omitting regular hooker Billy Clarey and switched prop Lou Hutt to the specialist role, with big Jack Arkwright being drafted into the blind side of the front row. Hutt was one of a trio of New Zealanders in the Saints' line-up – Roy Hardgrave and Trevor Hall were the others – while Arkwright was followed to Knowsley Road by his son Jack in the 1960s and grandson Chris in the 1980s. There was a nice touch from local rivals St Helens Recs when the Saints squad arrived at Station Road courtesy of a good luck telegram signed by Colonel Guy Pilkington and the City Road side.

Among moments to savour in the pre-match build-up was the Saints' mascot bedecked in red and white even though his favourites wore blue and white on the day. The youngster's jersey sported the number DJ1 – the first registration of a car in the town, owned by St Helens timber merchant Fred Brown! Respective captains George Lewis (Saints) and Jim Sullivan (Wigan) were both Welshmen and, as the final scoreline indicates, this Saints versus Wigan confrontation resolved itself into a classic war of attrition with the opening forty minutes point-less. Saints faced both wind and rain in this period, but nonetheless went close to scoring through legendary winger Alf Ellaby and stand-off Leslie Fairclough, a genius dubbed 'The Little Drummer Boy' during his army service at the time of The First World War.

'Golden Boot' Sullivan was uncharacteristically off-target with a couple of first-half penalty shots, but Wigan nevertheless set the scoreboard in motion in the 43rd minute, when loose forward Tom Sherrington touched down after Johnny Ring's kick-through deceived the covering Fairclough. Sullivan yet again failed to add the goal points, and fifteen minutes ticked by before Saints sent their faithful fans into raptures when Ellaby, Hall and scrum-half Groves carved out a try from Fairclough, which Lewis converted.

With just two points separating the two sides and twenty minutes remaining, Station Road was no place for the faint-hearted, and even more so when Sullivan's equaliser intervened, but the Twin Towers of Wembley still loomed large for Saints and Wigan when the final whistle blew. It is now a matter of history that Saints triumphed in the replay at Leigh on the following Wednesday, thus earning the right to tackle Widnes at the Empire Stadium.

Half time: 0-0

St Helens 5
 Try: Fairclough
 Goal: Lewis

Wigan 5
 Try: Sherrington
 Goal: Sullivan

St Helens v. Wigan

The St. Helens And Wigan Cup Battle.—By George Green.

A classic of 'grinding intensity' it may have been on that March afternoon at Swinton, with honours even. Yet as George Green's cartoon shows, the Saints produced one of their greatest-ever performances in the replay at Mather Lane, Leigh, some four days later, to defeat their old adversaries 22-10 and march into their first ever Wembley final. Unfortunately, opponents Widnes produced a major shock by beating Saints' 'Team of all the Talents' 10-3. Thereby hangs the great unpredictability of Rugby League's finest cup competition!

St Helens: C. Crooks; A. Ellaby, W. Mercer, G. Lewis (*captain*), R. Hardgrave; L. Fairclough, W. Groves; L. Houghton, L. Hutt, J. Arkwright, T. Hall, B. Halfpenny, R. Harrison.

Wigan: J. Sullivan (*captain*); J. Ring, T. Parker, R. Kinnear, L. Brown; S. Abram, A. Binks; F. Stephens, T. Beetham, W. Hodder, L. Mason, G. Dixon, T. Sherrington.

St Helens v. Huddersfield League Championship final

7 May 1932
Belle Vue, Wakefield
Attendance: 19,386
Referee: Mr F. Fairhurst (Wigan)

To be League Champions in Rugby League usually involved a 'top four' play-off, with two semi-finals and the final played at a neutral venue. The Saints came second in the league during the 1931/32 campaign, yet had the chance to become champions for the first time by defeating Yorkshire rivals Huddersfield in the final at Wakefield. St Helens, winners of the Lancashire League, would be without two key players, 'Superstar' winger Alf Ellaby and dynamic second-rower Albert Fildes, who had to depart for the Australian tour with the Rugby League Lions. Nevertheless, upwards of 2,000 Saints supporters had made the trip across the Pennines and gave a huge roar as the Red and Whites ran out onto the Belle Vue turf in their quest for double glory. St Helens won the toss and skipper George Lewis decided to play with the wind in their favour in the first half. Unfortunately, centre Tom Winnard failed to take advantage and missed two early penalty attempts. Yet persistent pressure by the Saints was soon to have its reward. Garvey got the ball from a scrum and shot through the flat-footed Yorkshire defence. He swerved round full-back Bowkett and as second-rower Tiffany tried a desperate cover tackle, he flipped the ball to Winnard in a superb demonstration of the scissors move and the centre scored a gem of a try in the corner, which was converted by Lewis. Huddersfield did their utmost to get in the game, but to no avail. Just before half time, Winnard found touch near the Huddersfield line and scrum-half Thompson was penalised for feeding. Lewis piloted the ball over the bar to give the Saints a seven-point lead.

Soon after the second half began, full-back Bowkett registered Huddersfield's first points with a drop-goal, but Lewis replied with another well-taken penalty after scrum-half Garvey had been obstructed following a kick ahead. The St Helens defence seemed to be coping admirably until Jones and Lewis let a high ball bounce between them and Walker rushed in to score for the Yorkshiremen. Bowkett missed the conversion and there was no further scoring in the match. Although the final quarter had been a particularly tense affair for Saints' players and supporters, it was absolute agony for committeeman Bill Simister. The milk dealer, originally from Cornwall, was a particularly nervous spectator and spent the time groaning with his head in his hands, fearing the worst. He had brightened up considerably, however, when George Lewis was presented with the trophy by Mr J. Wood, the secretary of the Rugby League, but a problem ensued! George could hardly be seen by the triumphant Saints' supporters. Huge second-rower Jack Arkwright soon put matters right. He took hold of his captain and with one solid heave put him and the cup safely on his broad shoulders.

As soon as the team returned to St Helens, they boarded an open motor coach and drove to Harry Ince's house. The former secretary, who was seriously ill, stood at his bedroom window with tears in his eyes as George Lewis showed him the cup and his team-mates sang their victory song 'Praise God from Whom all Blessings Flow'.

The Mayor, Alderman Hewitt, welcomed back the new League Champions in front of a wildly enthusiastic crowd in the Town Hall Square. Half an hour later, the team boarded their coach for a tour of the town, with George Lewis in front, proudly holding the silverware. It certainly had been memorable benefit season for the Saints skipper! Needless to say, the party ended up at the White Hart Hotel, where the cup was filled over and over again in triumph and hundreds must have had enormous 'sups' out of it! The following day at St

Half time: 7-0

St Helens 9
Try: Winnard
Goals: Lewis (3)

Huddersfield 5
Try: Walker
Drop goal: Bowkett

St Helens v. Huddersfield

Champions at last! The Saints line up in front of the Pavilion at Knowsley Road with the League Championship and Lancashire League trophies at the end of the 1931/32 campaign. From left to right, back row: Mr Jones (chairman), Mr Morris (vice-chairman), Tom Winnard, Jack Garvey, Jack Arkwright, Ben Halfpenny, Ebor Hill, Bob Atkin, Mr Houghton (treasurer). Front row: Bob Jones, Harry Frodsham, Walter Groves, George Lewis (captain), Bill Mercer, Roy Hardgrave, Jack Marsh. Wing-wizard Alf Ellaby and second-rower Albert Fildes were with the Great Britain touring party 'Down Under'.

Andrews Church in Denton's Green, Saints' supporters in the congregation smiled broadly as they sang a line from Psalm 149, 'Let the Saints be joyful with glory'. What could have been more appropriate!

St Helens: G. Lewis (*captain*); R. Hardgrave, W. Mercer, T. Winnard, R.E. Jones; H. Frodsham, J. Garvey; R. Atkin, D. Cotton, E. Hill, B. Halfpenny, J. Arkwright, W. Groves.

Huddersfield: L. Bowkett (*captain*); E. Mills, G. Parker, H. Walshaw, R. Walker; E. Thompson, E. Richards; J. Rudd, S. Halliday, H. Sherwood, H. Tiffany, T. Banks, H. Young.

St Helens v. Wigan Wartime Emergency League

26 December 1944
Knowsley Road, St Helens

Attendance: 7,000
Referee: Mr Stockley (Leigh)

Yuletide spirit was in short supply in this torrid clash, as Saints suffered a second defeat in 24 hours at the hands of the Old Enemy. Having lost 20-5 at Central Park on Christmas Day, the Saints were poised for revenge, leading 3-2 just before half time, but then disaster struck with the sending off of George 'Porky' Davies. The legendary prop had been involved in a set-to with his opposite number Ken Gee and was sent for the early bath following a difference of opinion with referee Bill Stockley. The subsequent second penalty goal by Billy Belshaw inched Wigan in front after Johnny King had touched down for the Saints. Dubbed 'Porky' because of his trade as a butcher, barrel-chested 6ft, 16st Davies was later alleged to have struck Mr Stockley and was suspended *sine die*, but further investigation revealed that the punch was thrown by a soldier home on leave! However, the scene was set for an even more turbulent second half which was destined to be of just 15 minutes in duration and although short-handed, Saints battled bravely. Wigan increased their lead to 7-3 with a try by Ernie Ashcroft.

Irrespective of venue, Saints-Wigan confrontations are not for the faint-hearted and the fuse was lit for the final flashpoint with the awarding of a bitterly disputed touchdown to Wigan's Jack Fleming. The incident was covered in detail by the *St Helens Reporter*, which stated: 'Balshaw's cross-kick was deflected by Saints captain Stan Powell, while his team-mate Jack Waring was badly obstructed by Jimmy Lowe, who then sent Fleming over with a blatant forward pass. Referee Stockley put his whistle to his lips and Saints stopped running in expecting him to blow. But he didn't and Fleming touched down between the posts, from where the official also acted as linesman in signalling its conversion. Mr Stockley was unwise in the extreme to position himself in close proximity to the Saints' section of the crowd, a number of whom had to be restrained from attacking the referee by the Saints' players.'

Such was the mayhem, the game had to be abandoned and Mr Stockley left the field under police protection. Saints were ordered to post warning notices on crowd behaviour for the remainder of the 1944/45 wartime season. So yet another Saints versus Wigan confrontation passed into rugby league folklore, while the local legend that was George 'Porky' Davies lived on until the grand old age of ninety before passing away at his daughter's home on the Isle of Skye.

On an environmental note, present-day supporters clamouring for a new stadium on the premise that Knowsley Road is past its sell-by date would really have had something to moan about in 1944. For, given wartime austerity and financial constraints, there was little or no concrete and steel construction at the time-honoured enclosure, which was then already more than fifty years old. Wooden stands flanked the touchlines and railway sleepers masqueraded as terracing, while an open expanse of banking at the Eccleston End was affectionately known as the Kop. Through this, a herd of cattle regularly meandered from the adjacent Holme Farm to ensure that the hallowed Knowsley Road turf was both fertilised and manicured. The scoreboard was positioned at the Boys' Pen End and was a ramshackle wooden monstrosity emblazoned with the names of the Saints and Visitors. The relevant scores were hung on strategically placed nails by a schoolboy who doubled in taking the chalked-up team changes board round prior to kick-off. Free admission and a programme (price one penny) was his reward. Team selection was very much a hit-and-miss affair, with

Half time: 3-4

St Helens 3
Try: King

Wigan 12
Tries: Ashcroft, Fleming
Goals: Belshaw (3)

St Helens v. Wigan

Saints' line-up as the Second World War was drawing to a close, with tearaway prop George 'Porky' Davies third from the right in the back row. The former Wigan Highfield and Liverpool Stanley front-rower was one of the most uncompromising forwards in the game and was always a big crowd favourite at Knowsley Road. The St Helens club carried on during the hostilities and actually took part in the Yorkshire Cup, together with rivals Wigan, for a spell.

players often recruited from the crowd via a loud hailer, while kit – or rather lack of it – was also a problem and improvisation was the watchword here, with flour bags being used as jerseys due to shortage of clothing coupons. Scrum-half Billy French was the trend-setter in this makeshift strip, on which 'self-raising' could be spotted by the more discerning eye.

St Helens: J. King; A. Gregory, J. Waring, F. Balmer, F. Riley; S. Powell (*captain*), F. Bowyer; G. Davies, F. Phillips, N. Thompson, Shaw, L. Higgins, E. Mills.

Wigan: W. Belshaw, J. Fleming, J. Lowe, J. Maloney, E. Ashcroft; M. Ryan, T. Bradshaw; K. Gee, J. Egan (*captain*), J. Featherstone, H. Atkinson, J. Cayzer, J. Blan.

St Helens v. Wigan Northern Rugby League

4 April 1947
Central Park, Wigan

Attendance: 30,000
Referee: Mr Cowell (Warrington)

'Wigan well-whacked!' The *St Helens Newspaper* made no bones about it after Saints pulled off a great against-the-odds win in this utterly compelling derby clash. The hard-earned victory was Saints' first at Central Park for 15 seasons and came in the wake of three successive post-war defeats versus the Old Enemy, who sat proudly at the top of the table, while Saints languished in the lower reaches after a disastrous first half of the campaign. In this dire period, the Knowsley Road side had lost 12 games in 21, including the opening six, and had seen fellow strugglers Liverpool Stanley achieve the double over them for the only time.

Something had to be done to stop the rot, particularly from a possession angle, and Saints moved to sign Vincent Dilorenzo, a ball-getting hooker from Bradford Northern who had previously played for Crosfields Recreation club in Warrington. But despite the capture of 'Dillo' and the recruitment of several rugby union stars from the Welsh valleys, Saints were quoted at 10-1 to win at Wigan, while a 20-point margin was a conservative forecast amongst the pundits either side of Billinge Lump. Small wonder that the local press later enthused: 'Superb Saints defied the Cherry-and-White hoodoo in cocking a snook at Wigan's hitherto long run of success, and wiped the derisive grin off the faces of Wiganers.'

Good Friday was a time of mixed fortunes for one Saint in particular, and that was strong-running second-rower Tommy Leyland, who scored the first try in the opening forty minutes, and then broke his collar-bone just into the second half. The blond-haired former schoolboy international was in considerable pain on the return journey but still managed a smile, as well he might after enjoying a major role in the Saints' form-book reversing upset. Like Wigan's stand-off Frank Tracey, Leyland was a product of the prolific Lowe House School 'nursery' and was a member of the Town schoolboy squad that embarked upon a trailblazing tour of France in 1935. Tommy hung up his boots while with Oldham and lived in the town well into his eighties and remained a familiar figure at Saints' past players' functions.

So, without doubt, Central Park 1947 provided the likeable Leyland with the highpoint of his career at Saints which, as with many of his team-mates, was shortened by the call of King and Country, and no-one more so than captain Jim Stott, who spent six years in khaki. Dubbed 'St James of Parr', Stott was partnered in the centre on this Saints' red-letter day by his younger brother Tommy, who was home on leave from the army. Jim's military classification was that of 'Craftsman' and he certainly merited that grading on the rugby field. Blessed with an uncanny ability to read a game, pivotal figure Jim rallied his troops after Wigan had threatened to storm to a runaway victory with a try as early as the third minute, which was scored by New Zealander Brian Nordgren and created by his fellow countryman Cecil Mountford.

Saints' initial response came via the former Pontypool stand-off and Royal Navy Lieutenant Len Constance, who put winger Ernie Mills away, and when he was stopped, the Stott brothers carved out a gap for Leyland for Jim Stott to convert. One-time Llanelli scrum-half Glan Jones inched Saints into a 7-3 lead with a snap drop-goal, only for Wigan full-back Johnnie Lawrenson to reduce his team's arrears with a penalty goal when Saints wandered offside.

What was to prove the crucial try for Saints arrived just before half time at a point when

---

Half time: 12-5

St Helens 12
Tries: Leyland, Pimblett
Goals: J. Stott (2)
Drop goal: Jones

Wigan 7
Try: Nordgren
Goals: Lawrenson, Mountford

St Helens v. Wigan

A stunning vista from pitch level during the Saints-Wigan clash at Central Park as the ball shoots out from the scrum. Saints' players (wearing orange and brown-hooped jerseys) are Leyland, Jones, Constance and Mills.

Nordgren and Mountford had dribbled deep into Saints' territory. But the visiting full-back Harry Pimblett was Saints' hero of the hour with a brilliant pick-up before feeding Jim Stott on half-way, and he was then up in support to take Jim's return pass and romp over. Pimblett's touchdown in the corner was hotly disputed by Wigan fans, who contended that Harry had failed to ground the ball properly in a double tackle by Johnnie Lawrenson and Stan Jolley. However, referee Paul Cowell allowed the try after consulting the linesman. Jim Stott tacked on the conversion from wide out to give the Saints a 12-5 cushion on the turn-round and the question on every Saints' supporter's lips was 'Is it enough?' Happily, their fears were unfounded as a 12-man Saints' team facing far from spring-like weather revealed defensive resolve of Rorke's Drift dimensions in restricting thoroughly wound-up Wigan to a Mountford penalty goal, which were the only points of a dour second half. So it was a happy Easter for both Jim Stott's men and the thousands of ecstatic supporters who made their way home through the 'no-man's land' of Billinge. Honour had at last been restored against the Old Enemy!

St Helens: H. Pimblett; D. Greenall, T. Stott, J. Stott (*captain*), E. Mills; L. Constance, G. Jones; W. Norris, V. Dilorenzo, R. Roughsedge, T. Leyland, H. Lewis, J. Dixon.

Wigan: J. Lawrenson; B. Nordgren, C. Mountford (*captain*), E. Ashcroft, S. Jolley; F. Tracey, T. Bradshaw; K. Gee, J. Egan, G. Banks, F. Barton, H. Atkinson, W. Blan.

St Helens v. Huddersfield Championship semi-final

2 May 1953
Knowsley Road, St Helens

Attendance: 21,000
Referee: Mr Hill (Dewsbury)

'Come home, all is forgiven!' was the joyful welcome from ecstatic Saints' fans after this incredible act of deliverance from a Huddersfield ghost that had haunted them for the past seven days. For on the previous Saturday, the rank outsiders had defeated League leaders Saints 15-10 in the Challenge Cup Final at Wembley – revenge was in the air! And so it proved, but never in their wildest dreams did the Knowsley Road faithful expect captain Doug Greenall's side to atone with a 10-try, 8-goal whitewash of the cup holders, which gave Saints their biggest victory in a Top Four play-off.

'Who can weigh up a team capable of two such contrasting performances in such short a time?' wrote a perplexed but delighted 'Premier' (Tom Reynolds) in the *St Helens Reporter*. 'It seems to me it is one of the sometimes fatal fascinations that Saints cast around themselves.' Or, as Saints chairman Harry Cook succinctly put it: 'You may not know what Saints will do next, but they certainly keep your heart palpitating. If it is excitement you want, it is excitement you get from watching Saints.' Some things never change!

Suggestions that Huddersfield were 'tired' due to playing an outstanding league game in midweek should have been discounted, because they fielded a reserve-packed thirteen. It is nearer the truth to state that the Fartowners were exhausted at the final whistle in attempting to cope with a Saints' squad imbued with flair and free-flowing rugby at its best. The hat-trick hero of the hour for Saints was former Newport and Abertillery second-rower George Parsons – on the same day that soccer maestro Stanley Matthews won his only Cup Final winner's medal for Blackpool against Bolton Wanderers at Wembley. The lantern-jawed Parsons, of the long, loping stride, could not have failed to impress on-looking Great Britain selectors, as indeed must fellow sons of the Principality Don Gullick and Ray Cale, who both originated from Pontypool. The former policeman George signed for Saints in 1948 along with another Abertillery star in winger Stewart Llewellyn. They made a joint debut versus Rochdale Hornets at Knowsley Road, with Saints losing 9-8 on a day when they were reduced to twelve men after full-back Albert Butler broke his collar-bone. Parsons enjoyed a somewhat dubious distinction in being awarded his Welsh cap in 1991 – forty-three years after winning it! For twenty-one-year old George was taken off the train en route for France in 1948 for 'daring' to talk with Saints' officials.

However, determined to reverse their eclipse at Wembley, Saints brought in half-backs Peter Metcalfe and John 'Todder' Dickinson in place of Jimmy Honey and George Langfield for the action replay with Huddersfield, who lacked the injured Pat Devery and Jack Large, with Dick Cracknell and Jim Cooper coming into the visitors' line-up. The Saints' switch ordered by coach Jim Sullivan turned up trumps, as former Pilkington Recs product Metcalfe and teenager Dickinson soon asserted their authority over Lance Todd Trophy winner Peter Ramsden and Billy Banks, who led the Saints a merry dance at Wembley.

Formidable centre duo Greenall and Gullick thrived on the creative skills of the new half-back pairing, which had much to do with Saints being home and dry in leading 28-0 at half time, including half a dozen tries from the top drawer. These were scored by Parsons, with two; Glyn Moses; Greenall; Cale and 'Showman' Stan McCormick, whose enormous sidestep and baffling change of pace saw him beat Peter Henderson and

Half time: 28-0

St Helens 46
Tries: Parsons (3), Moses, Llewellyn, Gullick, Greenall, McCormick, Dickinson, Cale
Goals: Metcalfe (8)

Huddersfield 0

St Helens v. Huddersfield

Bewitched, bothered and bewildered! Huddersfield winger Peter Henderson is unceremoniously brought to ground by Saints' centre-wing combination Don Gullick (left) and Stan McCormick. St Helens went on to lift the Championship trophy with a convincing 24-14 victory over Halifax at Maine Road, Manchester, a fortnight later in front of over 50,000 fans!

Johnnie Hunter on a 50-yard dash to the try-line.

Metcalfe tacked on four conversions and there was little respite for bewitched, bothered and bewildered Huddersfield after the interval. For slick-handling Saints added another four touchdowns from Llewellyn (courtesy of a McCormick cross-field break), Gullick (who blasted Hunter from his path), and Parsons to complete his hat-trick...and it fell to Dickinson to notch the last try. Metcalfe's trusty boot saw him finish with eight goals to set the seal on a Saints' display which Knowsley Road greybeards enthuse over to this day!

St Helens: G. Moses; S. Llewellyn, D. Greenall (*captain*), D. Gullick, S. McCormick; P. Metcalfe, J. Dickinson; A. Prescott, R. Blakemore, G. Parr, G. Parsons, W. Bretherton, R. Cale.

Huddersfield: J. Hunter; P. Henderson, R. Pepperill (*captain*), L. Cooper, D. Cracknell; P. Ramsden, W. Banks; E. Slevin, G. Curran, J. Bowden, J. Brown, J. Cooper, D. Valentine.

St Helens v. Wigan Lancashire Cup final

24 October 1953
Station Road, Swinton

Attendance: 42,793 (record)
Referee: Mr Coates (Pudsey)

Maybe it's a hackneyed cliché, but if ever a game was a tale of contrasting halves, then this first county cup showdown between the arch-rivals was it! For the Central Park side flattered to deceive in leading 8-4 at the interval, but faltered badly later on when a Saints' squad, now finding its touch, rallied to score twelve unanswered points. With both teams scoring two tries apiece, goalkicking, or lack of it in Wigan's case, proved the deciding factor and Saints had an ace up their sleeve in stand-off Peter Metcalfe, who landed five goals from six attempts, while Ken Gee and Tom Horrocks could only manage one from eight. The lifting of the trophy by Captain Doug Greenall was only Saints' second success in the Lancashire Cup competition, with the previous one being versus St Helens Recs in 1926. Wigan were poised for a 14th appearance in the final on that balmy day in 1953.

Overall, this mouth-watering confrontation lacked nothing in sheer excitement and pulsating drama, which had the record gate of 42,793 on tenterhooks. However, with due deference to Metcalfe's trusty boot, it was his half-back partner Jimmy Honey who stole the show for Saints, although he might not have had the chance, for it was charismatic coach Jim Sullivan's plan to select the seasoned Joe Ball had the pitch been heavy. Normally a stand-off, pencil-slim scrum-half Honey scored a crucial try that gave Saints a lead they did not surrender in the second half. Jimmy then 'made' one for full-back Glyn Moses which was disallowed, and he generally caused Wigan all manner of problems in midfield throughout. Saints had defeated Barrow, Swinton and Warrington on their way to this compelling Lancashire Cup decider, and, having lost the toss for choice of strip, appeared in light blue instead of their traditional red and white. The early signs were ominous for the men from Knowsley Road, and it was 'eleven stone wringing wet' skipper Doug Greenall who set an inspiring defensive example by first stopping 17 stone Nat Silcock in full flight and then tracking down elusive Johnny Alty. Gee missed two highly-kickable penalties in a torrid opening 10 minutes, and it was somewhat against the run of play when Metcalfe gave Saints a 2-0 advantage with a 30-yard shot. But Wigan were not to be denied as Jack Broome and Jack Fleming engineered a try for ex-Saints back-rower Harry Street. Horrocks suffered a similar fate to Gee with a goal kick, as the ball bounced half a dozen times before reaching the posts! Again it was that man Metcalfe who showed Wigan how it was done by being on target when Gee fouled Alan Prescott after the two Test props had been eye-balling each other in an earth-shattering collision. Saints' tenuous 4-3 lead proved short-lived, however as, with half time beckoning, Alty broke from a scrum on half-way to send Fleming haring 30 yards to score, with the speedy Honey narrowly failing to overhaul the Wigan number six. The hapless Gee landed Wigan's sole conversion but, despite their four-point deficit, an air of quiet confidence continued to pervade Saints' dressing room during the half-time break. Metcalfe reduced Wigan's lead to 8-6 with his third penalty on the restart after the cherry and Whites had wandered offside. Then followed the dramatic intervention by Honey who, fed by Stan Mc. Cormick, outwitted Brian Nordgren, Jack Cunliffe and Broome before chipping ahead to plunge between the uprights. Metcalfe's conversion was a formality and, with Saints' fans at fever pitch, it came as no surprise against a tiring Wigan, when Greenall's Boys ensured the Lancashire Cup was bound for Knowsley Road when Moses touched down after wingman Steve Llewellyn had made the running. Metcalfe reached his nap-hand of goals via

Half time: 8-4

St Helens 16
Tries: Honey, Moses
Goals: Metcalfe (5)

Wigan 8
Tries: Street, Fleming
Goal: Gee

St Helens v. Wigan

A tale of two captains! Alan Prescott (left) and Duggie Greenall talk tactics at Knowsley Road. Greenall, a rugged centre, skippered the side against Wigan in the 1953 Lancashire Cup final, while Prescott went on to captain the club in their inaugural Challenge Cup success against Halifax three years later.

the woodwork before the champagne corks popped for a Saints' team celebrating the ending of a generation gap in County Cup matters, with the gleaming trophy a suitable stable-mate for the League Championship silverware on the Knowsley Road sideboard.

St Helens: G. Moses; S. Llewellyn, D. Greenall (captain), D. Gullick, S. McCormick; P. Metcalfe, J. Honey; A. Prescott, R. Blakemore, G. Parr, G. Parsons, W. Bretherton, V. Karalius.

Wigan: J. Cunliffe (captain); B. Nordgren, J. Broome, E. Ashcroft, R. Hurst; J. Fleming, J. Alty; K. Gee, R. Mather, N. Silcock, W. Collier, T. Horrocks, H. Street.

St Helens v. Barrow Challenge Cup semi-final replay

11 April 1956
Central Park, Wigan

Attendance: 44,731 (record)
Referee: Mr Coates (Pudsey)

Welsh international Stewart Llewellyn scored 240 tries in a nine-year career with Saints, but his epic touchdown in this Challenge Cup semi-final marathon has to be the most important of them all. The sides had drawn 5-5 in the first bite of the cherry at Swinton the previous Saturday, and then re-battled for 80 scoreless minutes before embarking on extra time of 15 minutes each way on a balmy Wednesday night in Wigan. Something had to give, but a further nail-biting nine minutes ticked by before the lithe 6ft winger from Abertillery provided an extra-special touch of brilliance which broke the deadlock and set Saints on the road to a third Wembley appearance.

The background to a tale of Boy's Own proportions for modesty-personified Llew was that his vital try came right out of the blue, and who better to re-live his greatest moment in a Saints' jersey than the star known throughout the Rugby League as Steve: 'I remember receiving a pass from Glyn Moses 80 yards out before handing off Barrow winger Frank Castle. I turned infield and evaded the covering Reg Parker and John 'Dinks' Harris and by this time castle had overtaken me, but I shook him off again and beat full-back Ted Toohey on the outside with 35 yards to go and then dived between the posts. The police had to rescue me from ecstatic team-mates and Saints' supporters. However, the real significance of the try only dawned on me when I called in the Grange Park Hotel that night and everyone wanted to buy me a drink!'

The abiding memory of the first eighty minutes of this action replay Saints versus Barrow blockbuster was of two ruthlessly relentless defences. Greybeard followers of Rugby League no doubt wracked their memories to recall such Herculean tackling stints from both sides. It was quite remarkable that mere flesh and blood could absorb so much punishment without once resorting to the 'magic sponge.'

Overall, this titanic penultimate step to Wembley glory was yet another classic of grinding intensity in the best Saints-Barrow tradition. Injuries caused both teams to make one change each from their line-ups at Swinton, with Ab Terry replacing Walter Delves in the Saints' pack, while Danny Leatherbarrow came in for Jimmy Lewthwaite on the Barrow right.

The opening exchanges set the pattern of what was to come with defences reigning supreme and, with attrition the keynote, it quickly became apparent that scoring would be at a premium – a typical cup-tie, in fact. From a try standpoint, there were near-misses in the first half by Leatherbarrow and Frank Carlton of Saints, while the Shipbuilders' skipper and marksman Willie Horne and Austin Rhodes of St Helens also failed to end the stalemate with several penalty attempts. The territorial pendulum swung markedly in Barrow's favour in the second half but, with Vint Karalius and Nat Silcock having 'blinders' upfront, Saints' defensive resolve proved equally as unyielding as that of barrow in the first 40 minutes. So it could be said that Llewellyn's incredible intervention was both timely and somewhat against the run of play, but on such strokes of inspiration are sporting contests won and lost – particularly Rugby League semi-finals, with Wembley the ultimate prize. Rhodes converted 'Llew's' try before Horne opened Barrow's account with a penalty goal to reduce Saints' lead to 5-2 at the extra-time interval and the men from Knowsley Road removed any lingering doubts of the outcome with their second try by George Parsons, after the Welsh forward's drop-goal attempt rebounded off Bill Healey.

After extra time. Normal time score: 0-0

St Helens 10
Tries: Llewellyn, Parsons
Goals: Rhodes (2)

Barrow 5
Try: Grundy
Goal: Horne

St Helens v. Barrow

The Saints line up for the photographer prior to their replayed semi-final clash with Barrow on a Wednesday evening at a packed Central Park. From left to right, back row: S. Llewellyn, G. Parsons, A. Terry, N. Silcock, G. Moses, V. Karalius, D. Greenall. Front row: L. McIntyre, A. Prescott (captain), J. Dickinson, W. Finnan, A. Rhodes, F. Carlton.

Rhodes rounded off Saints' scoring with the conversion while, valiant to the end, Barrow notched a last-gasp consolation try by St Helens-born Jack Grundy before celebrations of a Wembley date to come went on until the wee small hours in the Lancashire glass town. Needless to say, the toast was to Stewart Marshall Llewellyn who – the very next day – captained a reserve-riddled Saints' team to a 12-9 win at Workington and scored a try for good measure!

St Helens: G. Moses; S. Llewellyn, D. Greenall, W. Finnan, F. Carlton; J. Dickinson, A. Rhodes; A. Prescott (captain), L. McIntyre, A. Terry, G. Parsons, N. Silcock, V. Karalius.

Barrow: E. Toohey; D. Leatherbarrow, P. Jackson, D. Goodwin, F. Castle; W. Horne (captain), J. Harris; G. Woosey, V. McKeating, F. Barton, J. Grundy, R. Parker, W. Healey.

St Helens v. Halifax Challenge Cup final

28 April 1956
Wembley Stadium, London

Attendance: 80,000
Referee: Mr Lawrinson (Warrington)

The fifty-nine-year delay to lift the game's most prestigious trophy was finally over for Saints at last after this Wembley blockbuster – but it might have needed a replay! For dour, uncompromising Halifax held more adventurous Saints at bay for 66 minutes before an epic try from winger Frank Carlton ended the point-less impasse and one then sensed that the issue was decided. A Saints team hell-bent on consolidation added two further touchdowns versus a Thrum Hall squad exhausted by earlier defensive efforts, but who nevertheless contributed in full measure to an absorbing clash of styles. As ever on these cup final occasions, there was no shortage of pre-match drama, with the saddest sensation being that Saints' stand-off John 'Todder' Dickinson had to withdraw from the line-up due to a knee injury; he also missed the 1953 showdown against Huddersfield for similar reasons. 'I just couldn't run the risk of leaving the Saints with twelve men if I had to come off, because there were no substitutions then,' he remembers. 'I left the heart-breaking decision until the morning of the match,' added the former Parr Central schoolboy star.

The absence of Todder meant Saints had to reshuffle their middle backs, with centre Bill Finnan moving to stand off, with reserve Brian Howard taking Bill's place as partner to Carlton on Saints' left flank. The big Wembley date was local lad Howard's first Challenge Cup appearance after starring in RAF rugby union. There was also a fairy-tale story for homespun forward Roy Robinson. He was drafted into the Saints' pack at the eleventh hour as replacement for Walter Delves, who had been nursing an injury since the Championship semi-final, again versus Halifax.

'You could have knocked me down with a feather when coach Jim Sullivan told me at our Brighton Hotel that I was in the second row for my Challenge Cup debut,' said workhorse Robbie, a product of the St Helens Amateur League who was justifiably proud of his unexpected Wembley winner's medal. And, remembering their selection headaches, Saints could have been forgiven for thinking that there was a jinx on them because, amid the excitement of a third Wembley visit, they left their kit at Shaw Street railway station, which triggered frantic telephone calls before it surfaced at Euston. Panic reigned once more only two hours prior to kick off when the coach which was supposed to take Saints to Wembley from their hotel failed to arrive. A fleet of taxis was hurriedly summoned, but all's well that ends well as the coach suddenly appeared!

Saints defeated Warrington, Castleford, Bradford Northern and Barrow on their march to the Metropolis and an air of quiet confidence prevailed as they headed south, with the Maestro Sullivan convinced that Saints youth and speed would triumph against long-in-the-tooth Halifax. It was a hunch shared by Saints' fanatical supporters, more than 20,000 of whom packed the Wembley enclosure after boarding 17 special trains at Shaw Street or taking to the open road in motor coach or private car.

Resplendent in time-honoured red and white strip embellished with the Town coat of arms, Saints were soon to discover that Halifax were intent upon placing their faith in their 'Terrible Six' forwards, who were led by redoubtable Jack Wilkinson and former Bradford Northern warrior Ken Traill. Merciless tackling, the customary 'softening up' and safety first rugby epitomised the opening stanza, which was often par-for-the-course when these inter-

---

Half time: 0-0

Lance Todd Trophy: A. Prescott (St Helens)

St Helens 13
 Tries: Carlton, Llewellyn, Prescott
 Goals: Rhodes (2)

Halifax 2
 Goal: Griffiths

St Helens v. Halifax

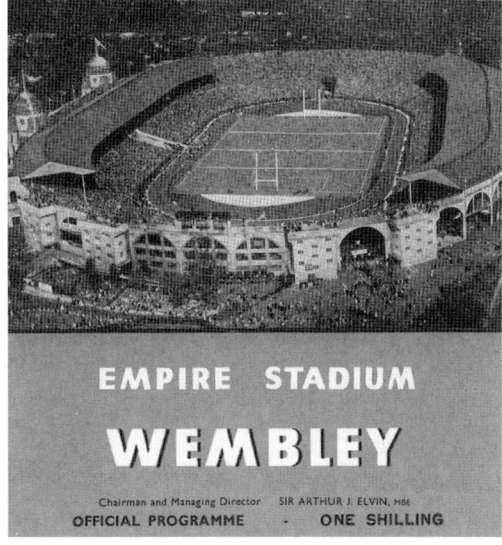

county rivals eye-balled each other. Not pretty, but it set the stage for a gripping, no nonsense first sixty-odd minutes.

Straight from the kick-off, Saints' inborn handling skills hinted of more fruitful times ahead and they almost drew first blood when Nat Silcock and Carlton sent Howard over, only for referee Ron Gelder to rule the final pass forward. Right winger Steve Llewellyn also crossed the Halifax line on the stroke of half time but broke touch en route and with Austin Rhodes and Tysull Griffiths failing with a succession of penalty kicks, there was little prospect of an end to stalemate at half time, with talk of a replay a recurring question at the Empire Stadium in 1956.

Despite coach Jim Sullivan's morale-boosting edict that victory was in sight for Saints if they moved the ball wide, skipper Alan Prescott's side continued to be drawn into a by now irksome arm wrestle on the restart, but, cometh the hour, cometh the man to spark the Saints' scoring machine into life. It fell to the colossus Prescott to raise the siege on Saints' line and supply massive psychological uplift with a series of tremendous breaks.

It was one such sortie that led to the try that all St Helens had been waiting for. Full-back linked up at a scrum to allow Prescott and Vint Karalius to put Howard away and he drew

---

St Helens: G. Moses; S. Llewellyn, D. Greenall, B. Howard, F. Carlton; W. Finnan, A. Rhodes; A. Prescott (*captain*), L. McIntyre, N. Silcock, G. Parsons, R. Robinson, V. Karalius.

Halifax: T. Griffiths; A. Daniels, T. Lynch, G. Palmer, J. Freeman; K. Dean, S. Keilty; J. Wilkinson, A. Ackerley (*captain*), J. Henderson, A. Fearnley, L. Pearce, K. Traill.

St Helens v. Halifax

Arthur Daniels in copybook fashion before feeding the thoroughbred Carlton. The Halifax line lay 60 yards in the distance, but the flying Frank swept round full-back Griffiths and outpaced the covering Johnnie Freeman to score at the side of the posts. Wembley erupted – at least the Saints' faithful did – before Rhodes tacked on his first goal and having at last made the initial penetration into a hitherto watertight defence, Saints then indulged themselves with a brace of Challenge Cup-clinching tries.

The first came when the powerful Silcock swatted aside Geoff Palmer and Freeman, prior to feeding Greenall, and Duggie timed his pass perfectly to send Llewellyn in at the corner. Rhodes added a superb goal before Griffiths landed a penalty for Halifax. Lance Todd Trophy winner Prescott then set the seal on an historic afternoon for Saints by plunging over by the corner flag following a break by Karalius and although Rhodes' conversion attempt rebounded from an upright it was of no consequence – the Challenge Cup was on its way to Knowsley Road.

Prescott and Jim Sullivan wept tears of joy as Earl Alexander of Tunis presented the silverware in front of an emotionally-charged Wembley crowd. Later on the saintly conquering heroes from the Glass Town returned to their Brighton hideaway and with it the acclaim of an army of ecstatic supporters. However, this mini-reception paled into insignificance by comparison with the welcome accorded the Saints on the following Monday night, when all police leave was cancelled as an estimated 20,000 overjoyed fans took over Victoria Square. The Wembley disappointments of 1930 and 1953 were forgotten as Saints' chairman Harry Cook told the happy throng 'At last we have given you what you wanted most.'

Not this time! Saints' first try hero Frank Carlton is halted by the Halifax cover defence. Halifax forward Albert Fearnley is on the left. Other Saints players in the picture include Austin Rhodes, Alan Prescott, Brian Howard, Vince Karalius and Roy Robinson.

ST HELENS v. HALIFAX

The 59-year wait is over. Skipper Alan Prescott is held aloft by his jubilant team-mates after Saints' first-ever Challenge Cup Final success. From left to right, back row: Roy Robinson, Len McIntyre, Vince Karalius, Alan Prescott, Nat Silcock, Bill Finnan, Steve Llewellyn, George Parsons. Front row: Brian Howard, Frank Carlton, Glyn Moses, Duggie Greenall, Austin Rhodes.

The celebrations went on unabated a couple of miles from the Town Hall in buntingbedecked O'Sullivan Crescent, Blackbrook, where Frank Carlton, whose try broke the deadlock, was given a rapturous return home by neighbours, while his proud mother could only utter 'I'm glad he didn't knock on!' On a financial note, it was estimated that the business life of St Helens was £150,000 poorer because of Saints' supporters pilgrimage to Wembley. But the consensus was that it was a small price to pay when set against the sheer jubilation of the frenzied fans in their team's moment of glory.

As a postscript, a thumbnail appraisal of the thirteen history-making Saints at Wembley in 1956 might read something like this: Glyn Moses – game of his life; Steve Llewellyn – wing artiste; Doug Greenall – crash-tackler supreme; Brian Howard – youngster who had a great understanding with his winger; Frank Carlton – most dangerous winger on the field; Bill Finnan – tremendous on attack and defence; Austin Rhodes – great performance and unfazed by early goal missed due to tricky cross-winds; Alan Prescott – mighty man who regularly 'took on' Wilkinson and company; Len McIntyre – gave Saints a possession pull and lively in open play; Nat Silcock – underlined that prop is his best position; George Parsons – brainiest forward on the field; Roy Robinson – a rising star without doubt; Vint Karalius – wonderful skills from spade-like hands. Carve their names with pride indeed!

St Helens v. Australia Tour Match

24 November 1956　　　　　　　　　　Attendance: 17,100
Knowsley Road, St Helens　　　　　　　Referee: Mr Smith (Barrow)

'Caps the lot!' That was the unanimous view of euphoric Saints' supporters after this record 10-try slaughter of the hapless Aussies by skipper Alan Prescott's charges. The unexpected victory – and its margin – was all the more remarkable because the team had been in the doldrums of late, but the scintillating Saints played like men inspired to earn a third successive win over mighty Australia. Almost at full strength, the men in the green and gold strip wilted and then crumbled in the face of wave after wave of breath-taking attacks such as few international squads ever encounter. Greater teams than they would not have stemmed the tide that finally engulfed them from a Saints' thirteen who were simply unstoppable. It was without doubt vintage rugby league that rocketed the Knowsley Road side back into the forefront of the British game, with the consensus being that the team be selected en-bloc for the Second Test versus Australia! Qualification for a Great Britain jersey would not have been a problem, for the soaraway Challenge Cup holders line-up comprised eight locals, three Widnesians and two Welshmen.

Magnanimous as ever, proud Prescott later said: 'Time was slipping by for Saints and, with five defeats so far, we were losing ground in the league. With no Championship points at stake, Saints felt they could treat the Australian fixture almost as a trial game and throw the ball about with abandon. Everything went right for us on the day and it was the best display from a Saints' side that I could remember. It could prove the turning point of the season.'

But *St Helens Reporter* scribe 'Boffin' preferred to take a more temperate view in writing: 'The Australians ranked among the poorest touring sides to visit these shores. Many of their faults were elementary ones which should have been corrected at schoolboy level, and certainly not when the player attained international status. On this showing the Australian selectors must have regretted leaving stars of the calibre of Rex Mossop, Tony Paskins and Johnny Mudge kicking their heals on Sydney's beaches. However, nothing should detract from a truly magnificent performance by a super-fit Saints side that fielded one of its biggest-ever packs of forwards, at the base of which half-backs John 'Todder' Dickinson and Austin Rhodes provided the ideal fulcrum to a superbly fluent back division. As well as a triumph of teamwork, this saintly extravaganza was also an afternoon of individual heroics when every member of the pack crossed the Australian line, while marksman Rhodes amassed 17 points with seven goals and a try. Saints were firmly in the driving seat by half time courtesy of touchdowns from Steve Llewellyn, Josh Gaskell, Frank McCabe and Nat Silcock, with Rhodes on target with three conversions. The rout raged unabated on the restart, with further tries from Vint Karalius, Dickinson, Llewellyn again, Rhodes, Ab Terry and Prescott. Rhodes landed four more goals.

A somewhat chastened Kangaroo party enjoyed some consolation at the Town Hall reception, when the sporting manner with which they had accepted defeat was remarked upon by Saints' vice-chairman Cecil Dromgoole, who was deputizing for the indisposed Harry Cook. The time-honoured presentations of glassware followed in the wake of a trouncing in which, sadly, performing of their war-cry was probably the only time the Australians moved in unison!

Half time: 18-0

St Helens 44
Tries: Llewellyn (2), Gaskell, McCabe, Silcock, Karalius, Dickinson, Rhodes, Terry, Prescott
Goals: Rhodes (7)

Australia 2
Goal: Clifford

ST HELENS v. AUSTRALIA

Saints PROGRAMME

Published by the ST. HELENS RUGBY F.C. LTD.

Directors: H. B. COOK (Chairman), C. DROMGOOLE (Vice-Chairman), W. BARTON, S. HALL, J. HARRISON, J.P., A. S. HOUGHTON, H. J. HUNTER, Coun. C. MARTIN, J.P., A. NAYLOR, L. SWIFT, F. YEARSLEY, J. YEARSLEY. J. A. ROBINSON, Company Sec. B. LOWE, Club Sec.

KEEP IN TOUCH
with
SAINTS
TOBACCOS
PETER DEWAR LTD.

Tel. 3693   Tel. 3693
51 CHURCH STREET
21 ORMSKIRK STREET   20 BRIDGE STREET

F. FLYNN, M.P.S.
THE CHEMIST

155 DUKE STREET, ST. HELENS

Asthma Inhalers, Baby Requisites, Dressings (as supplied to the Saints) Elastic Knee Caps, Anklets, Stockings, Litesome Belts, Patent Medicines, etc.

Telephone 3898

Saints second-rower Josh Gaskell in front of the old grandstand during a training session at Knowsley Road. A local product, Josh was a member of the St Helens' pack who all scored a try against the visiting Kangaroos – a measure of the team's desire to move the ball about during the match. Despite pleas to retain the Knowsley Road forwards en bloc for the Test matches, only Great Britain skipper Alan Prescott was selected. However, Saints' full-back Glyn Moses did make an appearance in the final Test Match, when Great Britain beat Australia 19-0 at Swinton on 15 December to win the series by a 2-1 margin.

St Helens: G. Moses; S. Llewellyn, D. Greenall, W. Finnan, F. Carlton; J. Dickinson, A. Rhodes; A. Prescott (captain), F. Mc. Cabe, A. Terry, N. Silcock, J. Gaskell, V. Karalius.

Australia: G. Clifford; D. Flannery, A. Watson, R. Poole, D. Adams; R. Banks, K. Holman; B. Davies, K. Kearney (captain), R. Bull, W. Marsh, D. Furner, T. Tyquin.

St Helens v. Leeds Northern Rugby League

26 October 1957
Knowsley Road, St Helens

Attendance: 23,000
Referee: Mr Harrison (Horbury)

There have been many stirring clashes with Leeds at Knowsley Road over the years, but for the 23,000 who packed the terraces on an autumnal afternoon this game had a particular significance. For this was the day when legendary South African winger Karel 'Tom' Van Vollenhoven wore a Saints' shirt for the first time and the team marked the momentous occasion by handing the Loiners a lesson in all that is best in rugby league football. Fresh from his rugby union triumphs against the British Lions (a hat-trick in opposition to Irish maestro Tony O'Reilly and five tries in three tests) 'Vol' was accorded a rapturous welcome by a discerning St Helens crowd. Ideally built for a wingman at 5ft 10in and 12st, the 22-year-old blond and crew-cut former Pretoria policeman was signed by the Saints in the face of intense competition from Wigan and Warrington.

Three tries by teenage scrum-half Alex Murphy put Saints on the way to a resounding success, with the other touchdowns coming from Brian Howard, Doug Greenall, Ray Price and Austin Rhodes (who also kicked six goals), before the try fans had waited patiently waited for was delivered. The final seconds were ticking away when stand-off Price sliced through the Leeds defence to serve Van Vollenhoven 40 yards out and the Springbok outpaced his 'policeman', George Broughton and full-back Jimmy Dunn to score at the Scoreboard End. Knowsley Road erupted on witnessing the first of Vollenhoven's 392 tries in 409 appearances up to 1968 for Saints, in the process of which he passed Alf Ellaby's total of 280 and also his seasonal best of 50 when Vol finished with 62 in 1958/59.

Totally besotted supporters marvelled at Vollenhoven's gazelle-like speed and fully understood his lack of rugby league know-how when he failed to make dead a kick-through which led to former British Lion Pat Quinn scoring Leeds' only try. The Knowsley Road faithful also applauded Tom's sportsmanship and hailed the try with a roar as full-throated as the response to Frank Carlton's winner at Wembley in 1956 and Steve Llewellyn's semi-final masterpiece at Wigan in the same year. It was inevitable that an ear-splitting seal of approval was accorded at full time to a wingman extraordinary, whose consummate artistry elevated him to bench-mark status for succeeding generations. Writing in the *St Helens Reporter* at the time, rugby league scribe Tom Ashcroft stated that Vollenhoven had left no doubt as to his try-scoring potential, both in range and total – a study of Tom's career would confirm the accuracy of that prophecy. Still finding his feet in the thirteen-a-side code, Vollenhoven was 'dropped' into the Reserve side a week later against Whitehaven at Knowsley Road. Such was his drawing power, a record 8,500 crowd saw him oblige with two superb long-distance tries. Vol had well and truly arrived!

Half time: 13-0

St Helens 36
Tries: Murphy (3), Rhodes, Howard, Greenall Price, Van Vollenhoven
Goals: Rhodes (6)

Leeds 7
Try: Quinn
Goals: Dunn (2)

St Helens v. Leeds

Fast forward to a marvellous St Helens victory over Leigh in the 1963 Lancashire Cup final at Station Road, Swinton. Tom Van Vollenhoven is about to touch down for try number 300 as a Saint! Tom played right centre in this match, a move – albeit temporary in nature – which sparked off controversy amongst St Helens fans at the time.

St Helens: G. Moses; T. Van Vollenhoven, D. Greenall, A. Rhodes, B. Howard; R. Price, A. Murphy; A. Prescott (captain), T. McKinney, A. Terry, N. Silcock, W. Delves, V. Karalius.

Leeds: J. Dunn; D. Hodgkinson, K. McLellan (captain), P. Quinn, G. Broughton; J. Lendill, J. Stevenson; A. Skelton, B. Prior, D. Robinson, C. Tomlinson, H. Street, C. Last.

St Helens v. Hunslet League Championship Final

16 May 1959
Odsal Stadium, Bradford

Attendance: 50,562
Referee: Mr G. Wilson (Dewsbury)

Ace South African wingman Tom Van Vollenhoven scored a record 392 tries for Saints, but his first of an eventual hat-trick in this points extravaganza was arguably the best of the lot! Picture the scene in this eagerly-awaited climax to the season: star-studded, but patently out-of-touch Saints find themselves 12-4 down after 25 minutes against unfashionable Hunslet, who had fully honoured their 'We've Swept the Seas Before' anthem. Enter Van Vollenhoven, courtesy of half-backs Alex Murphy and Wilf Smith, along with centre Doug Greenall, whose move from the scrum-base gave the former Springbok no more than just a ghost of a chance, two feet from touch and 75 yards out! Little did the massive crowd assembled on the dusty slopes of the Odsal amphitheatre on a stifling May day realise they were about to witness an epic try, arguably the best ever seen in a Championship Final!

To recapitulate: Greenall's deft pass saw Voll race away from Hunslet 'policeman' Willie Walker and then break the tackle of full-back Billy Langton on half-way. Covering defenders Brian Shaw, Jim Stockdill and Don Hatfield were left floundering by uncanny change of pace and sledgehammer hand-off before Tom majestically threaded his way to the Hunslet try-line. The try galvanised hitherto shell-shocked Saints into concerted action and with Austin Rhodes's goal meaning their deficit was now only 12-9, skipper Alan Prescott's men released the shackles to indulge in the free-flowing rugby which is Saints' birthright. The final score was a record in a Championship Final, as was the 10-goal tally of full-back Rhodes, who had switched from scrum-half only a fortnight previously following a knee injury to regular choice Glyn Moses.

A gallant Hunslet side that won at Wigan in the semi-final lacked nothing in guts and determination and had the consolation of scoring the highest number of points by a losing team, but simply could not cope with the speed and fitness of a now super-charged Saints. The Parksiders' early points came from tries by Stockdill and Kevin Doyle and three goals from Langton, who equalled the record of Jimmy Hoey of Widnes, a forward who scored in every match in the 1932/33 campaign.

Saints' opening salvo had been two penalty goals by Rhodes, but - spurred by Vollenhoven's timely intervention – they notched further tries from Murphy (2), Jan Prinsloo, Wilf Smith and Dick Huddart. Trailing 24-12 at half-time,

Half time: 24-12

St Helens 44
Tries: Vollenhoven (3), Murphy (2), Prinsloo, Smith, Huddart
Goals: Rhodes (10)

Hunslet 22
Tries: Stockdill, Doyle, Poole, Gunney
Goals: Langton (5)

St Helens v. Hunslet

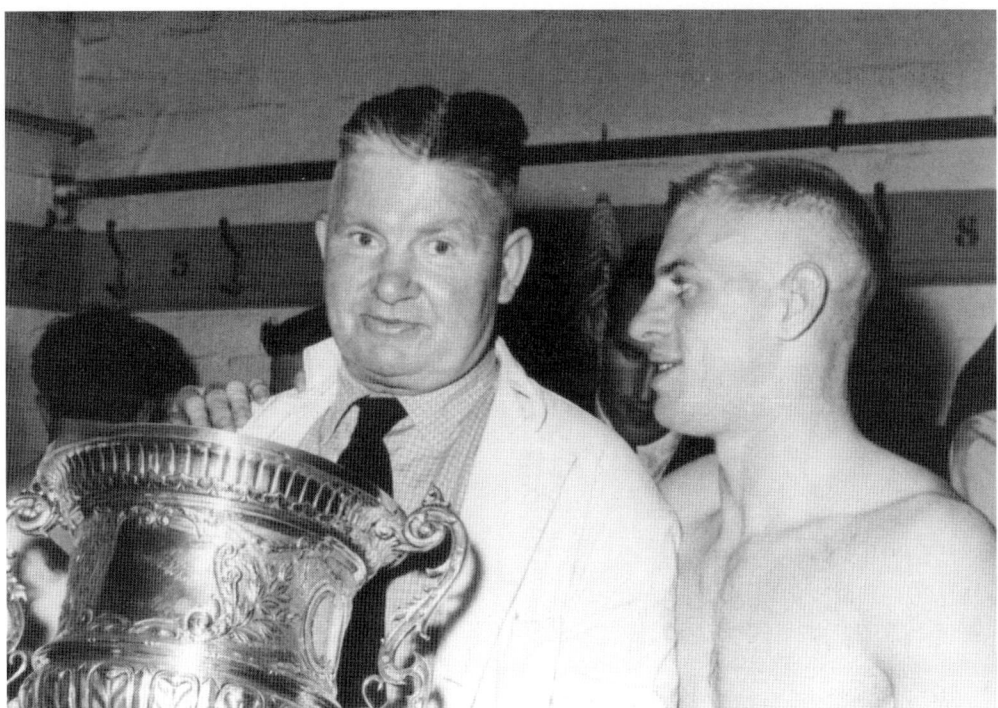

A partnership made in heaven! Coach Jim Sullivan and wing sensation Tom Van Vollenhoven get their hands on the Championship trophy in the dressing room at Odsal Stadium, Bradford.

Hunslet staunchly refused to buckle and were rewarded with touchdowns by Geoff Gunney and Harry Poole, with Langton tacking on both conversions to finish with a nap-hand of goals. Saints' Championship final triumph followed in the wake of those of 1932 and 1953 and did much to compensate for a Lancashire Cup final defeat versus Oldham and a second successive Challenge Cup defeat at Featherstone. Victory over Hunslet also set the seal on a season in which League leaders Saints amassed a record 1,005 points, while Vollenhoven's 62 tries surpassed the previous club best of 55 by Alf Ellaby.

After being chaired shoulder-high at Odsal, it was that man Vollenhoven who was also the target of Saints' supporters' adulation on the team's return to St Helens. 'We want Voll!' chanted the ecstatic throng assembled in Victoria Square. Yet the welcome home was no less deafening for the other twelve saintly heroes whose brilliant performance had captivated the entire rugby league world. And there was a fond farewell for legendary coach Jim Sullivan, who was taking up a new challenge at Rochdale. However, the abiding memory on that night to remember on the steps of the town hall was Tom Van Vollenhoven's departure for a well-earned holiday in his native Johannesburg – but only after he had assured the Knowsley Road faithful that he would return.

St Helens: A. Rhodes; T. Van Vollenhoven, D. Greenall, B. McGinn, J. Prinsloo; W. Smith, A. Murphy; A. Prescott (captain), T. Mc. Kinney, A. Terry, B. Briggs, R. Huddart, V. Karalius.

Hunslet: W. Langton; R. Colin, J. Stockdill, A. Preece, W. Walker; B. Gabbitas, K. Doyle; D. Hatfield, S. Smith, K. Eyre, H. Poole, G. Gunney, B. Shaw (captain).

St Helens v. Hunslet

The first of Tom Van Vollenhoven's three tries in the 1959 Championship final is considered to be a classic solo effort and was captured for posterity in a six-frame study by cameraman Robert Stiggins. Vol's run begins by swerving past the attempted tackle of Hunslet full-back Billy Langton, with loose forward Brian Shaw ready to cover the situation. Shaw is beaten and a third attempted tackle from centre Jim Stockdill is repulsed before Tom makes a successful touchdown. Notice the bandage on the left thigh, the result of a hamstring injury, which made him a doubtful starter for the game.

ST HELENS v. HUNSLET

Still an icon! Special guest Tom Van Vollenhoven signs autographs for fans before the St Helens versus Australia Ground Centenary match at Knowsley Road in September 1990 – some 32 years after that memorable Championship final against Hunslet. Needless to say, he was as popular as ever!

St Helens v. Hull Challenge Cup semi-final

19 April 1961
Odsal Stadium, Bradford

Attendance: 42,000
Referee: Mr Watkinson (Manchester)

Tactical awareness, allied to defensive resolve, and ultimately pace and handling skill, proved decisive as Saints set up a Wembley 'Final of the Century' with arch-rivals Wigan. A Hull side seeking a third consecutive trip to the Empire Stadium focused their game plan on scrum domination and keeping play tight, and that overtly insular policy succeeded in the first half hour when the Airlie Birds led 4-2. Something special was needed to break the deadlock, and it was forthcoming from South African winger Tom Van Vollenhoven, with an action replay of his epic touchdown against Hunslet in the same setting in 1959. The hint of a try was 'not on' when the Springbok took a pass from Don Vines deep in Saints' territory. But with powers of escapology bordering on the supernatural, 'Voll' evaded no fewer than six would-be tacklers on his way to the hull line.

That flash of inspiration gave hitherto struggling Saints a psychological uplift of a 5-4 lead at half time. It also lit the touch-paper for a five-try romp in the last forty minutes versus a Hull team that simply could not cope with Saints' ability to strike from long range. In a nutshell it could be said that Saints' surmounting of the penultimate Challenge Cup hurdle was a three-fold exercise: first by keeping the massive Hull pack at bay, then the recovery triggered by Van Vollenhoven and finally the victory march of ten points in as many minutes.

On a team selection note, Saints were without injured skipper Vint Karalius and seasoned hooker Bob Dagnall, with the side being led by prop Ab Terry, while up-and-coming hooker Dave Harrison wore the number nine jersey. Hull also had to make a change at hooker, where Jim Drake deputised for Test star Tommy Harris. At scrum-half was ex-Saints Tommy Finn, a product of St Austin's School, deep in the rugby league heartland of Thatto Heath. Prolonged drought and sunny conditions rendered Odsal a dust-bowl, but despite firm going ideal for open rugby, the opening stanza was one of rampaging Hull forwards led by Johnny Whiteley testing the mettle of the Saints' Six. Scrummaging offences also spelled a penalty-punctuated first twenty minutes, with Arthur Keegan's two-goals-to-one sway over Saints' Austin Rhodes allowing Hull's transported Threepenny Stand patrons a lung-bursting rendition of their time-honoured anthem 'Old Faithful'. However, it proved to be the only time they broke into song as – enter 'Mission Impossible' Van Vollenhoven – Saints assumed full control, with the carrot of a first-ever clash with Wigan in the Metropolis dangling before them. For, soon after the restart, the livewire Harrison carved out a try for Wilf Smith, then Captain Terry, Dick Huddart and Brian McGinn put Ken Large over in the corner, with Rhodes landing a magnificent conversion. More was to come from the now soaraway Saints as Alex Murphy, Vollenhoven and Mick Sullivan sent Rhodes racing across the Hull line with the Saints' full-back tacking on the goal. This was followed by a second try from Smith after another break by Huddart.

Murphy and Sullivan joined forces to create Saints' final try by McGinn, while a bewildered but gallant Humberside squad had to be content with a last-minute consolation touchdown by George Matthews. A six-to-one try ratio was testimony indeed to Saints' attacking superiority, while on a defensive note, former Dudley Kingswinford forward Cliff Watson ensured his Wembley call-up with an 80-minute tackling stint.

Half time: 5-4

St Helens 26
Tries: Smith (2), Vollenhoven, Large, Rhodes McGinn
Goals: Rhodes (4)

Hull 9
Try: Matthews
Goals: Keegan (3)

St Helens v. Hull

Below: Gamebreaker! Tom Van Vollenhoven's fantastic solo try that turned the tide against Hull at Odsal. 'Vol' left no less than six Hull defenders clutching thin air as he raced to the line. Saints' fans at ringside in the huge crowd have certainly started to celebrate in earnest!

St Helens: A. Rhodes; T. Van Vollenhoven, M. Sullivan, B. McGinn, K. Large; A. Murphy, W. Smith; A. Terry (captain), D. Harrison, C. Watson, D. Vines, R. Huddart, F. Terry.

Hull: A. Keegan; J. Kershaw, G. Matthews, S. Cowan, T. Hollindrake; F. Broadhurst, T. Finn; M. Scott, J. Drake, B. Hambling, C. Sykes, W. Drake, J. Whiteley (captain).

St Helens v. Wigan Challenge Cup final

13 May 1961
Wembley Stadium, London

Attendance: 95,000
Referee: Mr Watkinson (Manchester)

Given the proximity of St Helens to Wigan – eight miles as the crow flies over Billinge Lump – and their exalted standing in Rugby League, it is remarkable that 64 years elapsed before they clashed in a Challenge Cup final. This ultimate 'derby' on a sweltering hot day lacked nothing in cauldron-like atmosphere, individual flair and competitive edge, which are par for the course virtues when these arch-rivals lock horns. Superior speed and stamina were Saints' trump-cards in the energy-sapping heat, while the sponge-like, if hallowed, Wembley turf also took its toll on 26 heroes who gave their all over 80 gruelling minutes. And yet the destination of the Challenge Cup might easily have been the ancient township of Wigan, for the 'Colliers' had cause to rue missed chances in a game where the outcome hung in the balance until the 64th minute. Then, with Saints clinging to a 5-4 lead, Wembley's Empire Stadium was privileged to witness an epic try, which effectively sealed the issue and etched the name of Tom Van Vollenhoven into Knowsley Road folklore.

Just previously, Wigan's Fred Griffiths saw his penalty kick rebound from an upright while wingers Billy Boston and Frank Carlton were denied tries. A Saints' team under enormous pressure were forced to dropout from beneath the posts as St Helens-born captain Eric Ashton urged his men to snatch the initiative. Tragically for Wigan, the drop-out was fumbled by Brian McTigue and was seized upon by Lance Todd Trophy winner Dick Huddart. Alex Murphy took the play-the-ball and fed Ken Large, and he and Vollenhoven interpassed over 80 glorious yards before Tom touched down between the posts for Austin Rhodes to convert.

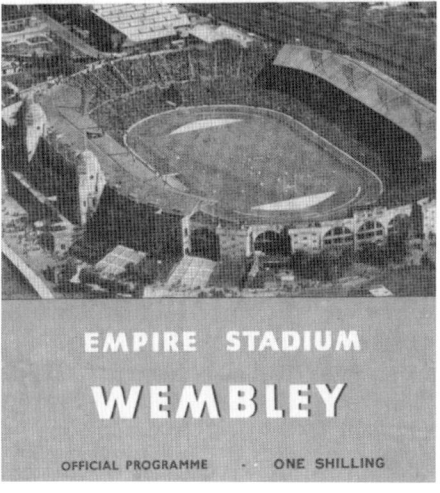

Earlier Wigan kicked off on a positive note when Griffiths landed a 4th minute penalty after Murphy wandered off-side, but Saints regained the advantage on the half-hour when Cumbrian Huddart broke the tackles of Terry Entwistle and Frank Collier to send Murphy scampering over. Rhodes failed with the goal kick, but made amends with a superb penalty from half-way when Geoff Lyon fouled Don Vines, and there was a note of cautious optimism from coach Alan Prescott as Saints adjourned to the 'lucky' North dressing rooms with a 5-2 lead at half time.

A second penalty by Griffiths after Wilf Smith was guilty of a 'feeding' offence inched Wigan to within a point of Saints on the restart. Then followed the Central Park side's three-pronged tale of woe prior to the Van Vollenhoven-Large intervention. Fifteen

---

Half time: 5-2

Lance Todd Trophy: R. Huddart (St Helens)

St Helens 12
 Tries: Murphy, Vollenhoven
 Goals: Rhodes (3)

Wigan 6
 Goals: Griffiths (3)

St Helens v. Wigan

Tense moments before kick-off as Cliff Watson, appearing in only his second Challenge Cup tie, is introduced to special guest Lord Derby. Vines and Huddart are next in line.

minutes still remained on the clock but, with Saints' skipper Vint Karalius outstanding and Bob Dagnall now ahead of Bill Sayer in the scrums, the rest, as they say, is history, with the only additions to the scoreboard being further penalties by Rhodes and Griffiths. Other points to ponder after this red letter day in the rugby league calendar might include the following cameos: Saints' hero Ken Large was only drafted in at the eleventh hour in place of John Donovan; ex-Dudley Kingswinford forward Cliff Watson was appearing in only his second cup-tie; Vollenhoven's try was his seventh in Saints' 1961 Challenge Cup saga; world's best scrum-half Alex Murphy played at stand-off. Add to all this the facts that respective left-wingers Carlton and Mick Sullivan were facing their former team-mates, while Rhodes and Karalius were the only survivors from the Saints' side that lifted the Challenge Cup for the first time in 1956.

However, probably the most illuminating statistic was that no fewer than sixteen of the participants were local to St Helens or Wigan. The seven Saints were: Rhodes, Large, Brian McGinn, Murphy, Smith, Ab Terry and Dagnall. Dyed-in-the-wool Wiganers were: Jeff Bootle, Dave Bolton, Entwistle, John Barton, Sayer, McTigue, Collier, Lyon and Roy Evans. How times have changed!

St Helens: A. Rhodes; T. Van Vollenhoven, K. Large, B. McGinn, M. Sullivan; A. Murphy, W. Smith; A. Terry, R. Dagnall, C. Watson, D. Vines, R. Huddart, V. Karalius (*captain*).

Wigan: F. Griffiths; W. Boston, E. Ashton (*captain*), J. Bootle, F. Carlton; D. Bolton, T. Entwistle; J. Barton, W. Sayer, B. McTigue, F. Collier, G. Lyon, R. Evans.

St Helens v. Wigan

Quick as a flash! Stand-off Alex Murphy leaves Wigan winger Billy Boston in his wake after scoring Saints' first try in the searing heat of the 1961 Cup Final.

The way we were! This ticket for the West Standing Enclosure at Wembley Stadium cost the princely sum of three shillings, or 15 pence! Spectators stood at both ends of the ground. In 1963, Wembley was given a £500,000 overhaul, making the stadium the only all-covered 100,000 capacity stadium in the world. By the 1990s, it had become a 79,000 all-seater stadium, including 56 executive boxes and 4,000 seats in the Olympic Gallery. The old stadium hosted its last Challenge Cup final in 1999. The Saints went on to play finals at Twickenham (2001) and Murrayfield, twelve months later. Yet nothing could match the magic of Wembley!

St Helens v. Wigan

The fruits of success! Goal-kicker supreme Austin Rhodes (centre) enjoys the moment with try-scorers Alex Murphy (left) and Tom Van Vollenhoven. The former Springbok's try, ably assisted by centre Ken Large, remains one of the greatest ever witnessed in a Challenge Cup final at Wembley.

St Helens v. Warrington Northern League Match

7 November 1964
Knowsley Road, St Helens

Attendance: 12,500
Referee: Mr Philpott (Leeds)

The Saints of the early 1960s were a formidable outfit who often took advantage of their 'Terrible Six' pack of forwards to grind their opponents into the turf. This, coupled with a steady stream of possession from hooker Bob Dagnall, gave them a platform to dominate matches. It might not have been pretty to watch but was certainly effective! One game against Warrington at Knowsley Road in the 1964/65 season, however, was a truly classic encounter, providing some scintillating rugby, moments of high drama and a story-book ending for Saints' man of the match Len Killeen. The South African wingman had taken on the kicking duties after Welsh full-back Kel Coslett had suffered a long-term injury earlier in the campaign. Len was a natural distance kicker and one of the first to place the ball upright – something taken for granted in the modern game. It was his two penalties that gave Saints breathing space in this see-saw struggle after Warrington came back to within two points at threequarter time. The first was a brilliant 45-yard effort from the Popular Side touchline. Warrington promptly failed to find ten yards with their restart kick and Lenny sent another towering kick between the sticks from the centre spot – absolutely soul-destroying for the opposition and the Saints were back in the ascendancy.

It was front-rower Cliff Watson who opened Saints' account on the twenty minute mark after receiving an inside pass from loose forward Duggie Laughton. Killeen converted comfortably. Warrington came back into the match with a Bootle penalty goal and a converted try from right-winger Melling, who picked up a loose ball and weaved through four defenders before touching down. There were two moments of controversy to follow – both fortunately going the way of the Saints! Wire scrum-half Gordon was penalised for delaying the put in at a scrum. Killeen duly added the two points to level proceedings at 7-7 and on the stroke of half time, Saints' skipper Alex Murphy raced onto a one-handed pass from big second-rower Merv Hicks and streaked over in the corner.

Referee Philpott dismissed the visitors' claims for a forward pass. Although Killeen's kick was wide of the mark, he made amends with another penalty shortly after the restart, but Warrington refused to lie down and hit back with Melling's second try. At 12-10 it was left to Killeen to calm jangling nerves with his two penalties, as the Saints' forwards bombarded the Warrington line in an effort to gain the breakthrough, which eventually came after big Cumbrian prop John Tembey barged his way over from short range.

Len Killeen, the superb all-round footballer and showman supreme was not finished yet! Tom Ashcroft in the St Helens Reporter was able to describe one of the longest tries ever seen at Knowsley Road which set the seal on a marvellous afternoon's entertainment: 'He snapped up a bouncing ball behind him on the line and darted through the gap in front of him. His speed over the first 25 yards into an open field was terrific. He sailed on to halfway without a falter and the question arose whether his stamina would withstand the call in the last 80 minutes of terrific football. Warrington had left the rear unguarded and the chief challenge came from little Gordon the scrum-half. The roar of the Popular Side reached a crescendo as the Rhodesian went on to win the great sprint. He touched down at the side of the posts and doubled up, utterly winded! Murphy had to take the goal-kick and Killeen came back to a gold medal reception on all sides.'

Half time: 10-7

St Helens 26
Tries: Killeen, Murphy, Tembey, Watson
Goals: Killeen (6), Murphy

Warrington 10
Tries: Melling (2)
Goals: Bootle (2)

St Helens v. Warrington

Below: The inimitable showman! Len Killeen makes a typically unorthodox attempt to score a try in a match against Wigan at Knowsley Road in 1964. Unfortunately, he had a hand in touch – but it was close!

St Helens: F. Barrow; T. Pimblett, K. Northey, W. Benyon, L. Killeen; P. Harvey, A. Murphy; J. Tembey *(captain)*, R. Dagnall, C. Watson, J. Warlow, M. Hicks, D. Laughton.
Subs: A. Barrow, R. French.

Warrington: G. Bootle; W. Melling, R. Fisher, J. Pickavance, B. Glover; W. Aspinall, P. Gordon; W. Payne, P. Donoghue, F. Hill, C. Winslade, M. Thomas, W. Hayes.
Subs: R. Greenough, H. Delooze.

St Helens v. Hull Kingston Rovers Championship semi-final

14 May 1966
Knowsley Road, St Helens

Attendance: 20,000
Referee: Mr Appleyard (Leeds)

Time-honoured Knowsley Road was no place for the faint-hearted as these inter-county rivals eye-balled in probably the most violent confrontation seen at the century-old stadium. The hard feeling was triggered by Saints' controversial last-minute victory over Rovers in the third round of the Challenge Cup at Knowsley Road a month previously. So it was a highly-incensed 'Robins' squad that came to St Helens intent on revenge, and it showed, with many unsavoury incidents being a danger to life and limb and certainly not within the Marquess of Queensbury's Rules. A clash that continued to degenerate throughout finally boiled over in the closing minutes when Saints' full-back Frankie Barrow floored his opposite number Cyril Kellett in an off-the-ball incident, sparking a mass brawl. Referee Appleyard decided that discretion was the better part of valour by blowing for time and, overall, reaching their second successive Championship Final had been the ultimate test of character for a Saints' team hit by injuries to Kel Coslett, John Warlow and Bob Prosser. Saints' pack leader Ray French said: 'Hull KR were totally focused on revenge and settling of old scores, which erupted straight from the kick-off. So I called our pack together and told them they had the option of lying down to this intimidation or facing up to it. With a Wembley date with Wigan on the following Saturday, it would have been easier to take the soft option, but the final result tells its own story, although there was only referee Appleyard and me not fighting at the end,' chuckled Ray. However, amid all the mayhem at Knowsley Road on a balmy night in 1966, there was one player who refused to become embroiled in what was going on all around him. That man was Saints' other South African winger Len Killeen. So often consigned to living in the shadow of the great Tom Van Vollenhoven, Killeen stole the show on this occasion by concentrating on the job in hand, a virtue which was rewarded as Len scored all Saints' points with two tries and four goals.

Second-rower French, who is now, of course, a respected media personality, also came of age as the Robins were put to flight, as did Barrow and Benyon in what was overtly a triumph of guts and determination. The first half general call-to-arms was inevitably punctuated by penalty awards, with Kellett on target with two attempts and Killeen one, which meant that Hull KR held a tenuous 4-2 lead at half time. Interval words of wisdom by Saints' coach Joe Coan had the desired effect after another Killeen penalty squared matters on the restart, for a surging break by French supported by

Half time: 2-4

St Helens 14
Tries: Killeen (2)
Goals: Killeen (4)

Hull Kingston Rovers 6
Goals: Kellett (3)

St Helens v. Hull Kingston Rovers

Little and Large! Saints' 'Mighty Atom' scrum-half Tommy Bishop is hoisted on high by pack leader Ray French during training for the 1966 Challenge Cup final. The Championship semi-final against Hull Kingston Rovers at Knowsley Road was one of the toughest faced by either player during their careers. The Saints went on to lift the trophy by swamping Yorkshire rivals Halifax to the tune of 35-12, at Station Road, Swinton. This was ample revenge for a St Helens side who had been defeated by the same opponents at the same venue, twelve months previously!

Benyon put Killeen between the posts to leave his conversion a formality. Given the grinding intensity of the dour struggle, Saints virtually booked their passage to the Championship final with a spectacular 80-yard touchdown by Killeen after he intercepted a pass from Frank Foster to Chris Young. Despite the lung-bursting chase, the nonchalant Len landed the touchline goal with considerable aplomb and the scoreboard was then redundant save for a third penalty goal from Kellett. But there was little let-up in the ferocious exchanges as illustrated by the Barrow-Kellett collision following the hoisting of a towering up-and-under by Saints' captain Alex Murphy. Happily, there were no further recriminations and cordial relations were quickly restored between Saints and Hull Kingston Rovers!

St Helens: F. Barrow; T. Van Vollenhoven, A. Murphy (captain), W. Benyon, L. Killeen;
R. Prosser, T. Bishop; A. Halsall, W. Sayer, C. Watson, R. French, J. Warlow, K. Coslett.
Subs: A. Barrow, G. Hitchen.

Hull Kingston Rovers: C. Kellett; C. Young, G. Wrigglesworth, J. Moore, R. Blackmore; D. Elliott,
A. Bunting; D. Tyson, P. Flanagan, P. Fox, W. Holliday, F. Foster (captain), T. Major.
Subs: R. Stephenson, A. Mullins.

St Helens v. Wigan Challenge Cup final

21 May 1966
Wembley Stadium, London

Attendance: 98,536
Referee: Mr H. Hunt (Lowton)

Glance at that scoreline and it is difficult to believe that Saints and their arch-rivals were level pegging before this eagerly awaited derby clash, which was their second meeting at Wembley Stadium. With Saints having won their first in 1961, the pundits' view was that Wigan were thirsting for revenge, but Saints' brilliant strategy and planning meant that the teams were poles apart at the final whistle. Wigan were without suspended hooker Colin Clarke and had to switch prop Tom Woosey into the specialist role, and Saints' captain Alex Murphy ruthlessly exploited his lack of experience against seasoned Bill Sayer – who was, ironically, a Wiganer! Murphy repeatedly found touch safe in the knowledge that Saints would regain possession from the ensuing scrum while, when Wigan had the ball, Saints were accused of offside tactics and the Cherry-and-Whites fell into the trap of also kicking for touch – and Saints had possession yet again. Even chief guest Prime Minister Harold Wilson commented on Saints' glut of possession, and it was no coincidence that the unlimited tackle rule was replaced by one of the four-tackle variety by the start of the 1966/67 campaign.

In a nutshell, Saints' huge pack ground Wigan down in the early stages before a speedier, more inventive back division took over. Saints also held several individual ace cards, in particular South African winger Len Killeen, who was a landslide winner of the Lance Todd Trophy with a try and five goals – one an incredible effort from fully 65 yards. One of the three South African wingers on view (Tom Van Vollenhoven and Wigan's Trevor Lake were the others), Killeen's nonchalant place-kicking rendered Wembley's allegedly tricky wind currents a figment of the imagination, or so it seemed. However, Leonard Michael Anthony Killeen would have readily conceded that Saints' surprisingly emphatic victory was no one man band performance. Rather, it was a masterpiece of organisation and execution orchestrated by the mercurial Murphy who reluctantly appeared in the centre instead of scrum-half.

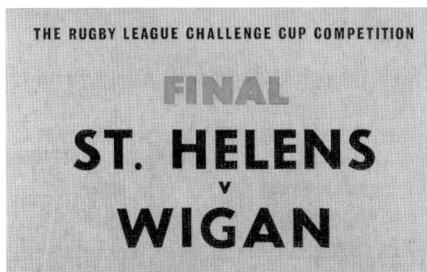

In the build-up to Saints' fifth Wembley visit coach Joe Coan prepared his squad on the gruelling Ainsdale sand dunes and the King George School fields at Southport, where the pitch was remarkably similar to the hallowed Wembley turf. Just how thoroughly Cumbrian Joe had done his homework might be gleaned by Saints' three-tries-to-nil ratio, plus another three disallowed, while woebegone Wigan

Half time: 9-2

Lance Todd Trophy: L. Killeen (St Helens)

St Helens 21
Tries: Mantle, Killeen, Bishop
Goals: Killeen (5)
Drop goal: Murphy

Wigan 2
Goal: Gilfedder

St Helens v. Wigan

Len Killeen about to launch another kick towards the Wigan posts. This time, he was unsuccessful, although Saints' South African superstar amazed the record 98,536 crowd with his penalty attempt in the 9th minute. This was the longest goal ever seen at the famous stadium in a Challenge Cup final – 65 yards out, five yards inside his own half and eight yards in from the touchline! Such an incredible piece of marksmanship clearly had a damaging effect upon the morale of opponents Wigan. Killeen went on to bag 13 points in the match, with 5 goals and a try, earning him the coveted Lance Todd Trophy. Yet he hardly received a pass all afternoon. His try came as a result of a grubber kick from his centre Bill Benyon! Killeen, with his golden boot, will always be remembered as one of the key players in what was a very one-sided final.

rarely threatened to open their account and remained try-less yet again versus Saints again at Wembley. All this before a record 98,536 crowd on a dry and sultry May afternoon in London in 1966. It was an ominous omen for Wigan when that man Killeen opened the scoring with a penalty goal when the Cherry and Whites, led by St Helens-born Eric Ashton, were caught offside. Wigan loose forward Harry Major was then penalised at the play-the-ball and, although Murphy and Killeen pondered over kicking for touch the rest, as they say, is history, as Len's long-distance howitzer found the target. A softening-up period of 17 minutes elapsed before Saints breached the Wigan line, with the chance coming after Albert

St Helens: F. Barrow; T. Van Vollenhoven, A. Murphy (*captain*), W. Benyon, L. Killeen; P. Harvey, T. Bishop; A. Halsall, W. Sayer, C. Watson, R. French. J. Warlow, J. Mantle.
Subs: A. Barrow, G. Hitchen.

Wigan: R. Ashby; W. Boston, D. Stephens, E. Ashton (*captain*), T. Lake; C. Hill, F. Parr; D. Gardiner, T. Woosey, B. McTigue, A. Stephens, L. Gilfedder, H. Major.
Subs: C. Hesketh, G. Lyon.

St Helens v. Wigan

Halsall, Tommy Bishop, Peter Harvey and Vollenhoven had made the running before John Mantle crashed over for Killeen to tack on the conversion. 'Voll' and Murphy then sent 'Pocket Battleship' Bishop between the Wigan posts, but the final pass was forward and Laurie Gilfedder then reduced the Cup holders' arrears to 9-2 via a 45-yard penalty goal after Saints had again wandered offside. Saints' tenuous half-time lead would have been reduced even further but for a magnificent last-ditch tackle by full-back Frankie Barrow on the lightning-legged Lake, who was heading for the corner after evading two tackles. Now holding a seven-point cushion and dominating the scrums, Saints were sitting pretty at half-time, but their off-side tactics triggered charges of gamesmanship from Wigan fans, who slow-handclapped Murphy and his men as they returned to the dressing rooms at the interval. Killeen kicked his fourth successive goal on the restart, when Wigan prop Danny Gardiner up-ended Billy Benyon after the Saints' centre kicked ahead and Harvey then had a try disallowed due to a forward pass from the rampaging Halsall. A strangely subdued Billy Boston,

You little beauty! Tommy Bishop's brilliantly taken 71st minute try, following a tantalising grubber kick into the heart of the Wigan defence. St Helens-born full-back Ray Ashby tries to avert the touchdown – without success. Saints scored two tries from kicks during the match, allegedly against the orders of Coach Joe Coan. Bishop, together with hooker Bill Sayer and prop Albert Halsall, were integral members of the side during the 1966 'Four Cups' season. Yet all three were only signed just before the Challenge Cup deadline!

St Helens v. Wigan

It's ours again! Skipper Alex Murphy is chaired by his jubilant team-mates after the demolition of the Old Enemy! Other players, from left to right: Bill Benyon, Len Killeen, Albert Halsall, John Warlow, Cliff Watson, John Mantle (hidden), Tommy Bishop, Ray French, Bill Sayer, Frankie Barrow and Tom Van Vollenhoven.

David and Tony Stephens and skipper Ashton all briefly posed problems for Saints as Wigan tried to spring back into contention, but lack of sustained team-work proved Wigan's Achilles heel as the Knowsley Road side moved in for the kill. Bishop lit the fuse with a brilliant break in the 54th minute before transferring to Benyon who, ignoring Coach Joe Coan's no-kicking edict, placed a perfectly weighted grubber to the corner. The Wigan defence was caught napping as Killeen's swallow-dive took him over by the flag for an unconverted try.

There was little sign of a let up from a Saints' team leading 14-2 as this one-sided Wembley showdown entered its final quarter. A powerful burst by Mantle saw Vollenhoven cross at the corner, but Tom had broken touch and a rapidly-tiring Wigan thirteen breathed again. But, in Wimbledon parlance, it was game-set-and-match with 71 minutes gone when, after Halsall and Benyon had set up position, Bishop enjoyed the rub of the green when his chip through ricocheted off Wigan's Haresfinch-born full-back Ray Ashby. 'Bish' was onto the loose ball in a flash and touched down between the uprights for Killeen to land his fifth goal. As if to rub salt into an already gaping wound, Wigan's tormentor-in-chief Murphy dropped a last-minute goal and thus ensured that the Central Park side suffered their heaviest defeat in a Challenge Cup final.

St Helens v. Halifax Championship final

28 May 1966
Station Road, Swinton

Attendance: 30,165
Referee: Mr J. Manley (Warrington)

High-flying Saints ended a record-breaking campaign in rousing style with this seven-try slaughter of the men from Thrum Hall – and made history for good measure. With the Challenge Cup, League Leaders and Lancashire League trophies already on the sideboard, lifting of the Championship 'pot' saw Saints join the exclusive clique who have won four cups in one season. Whit Saturday's gala performance made it a very merry month of May for skipper Alex Murphy's side, in what was a revenge mission after Saints' defeat by Halifax in the Championship final of 1965.

With Saints having surrendered their five-year grip on the Lancashire Cup earlier in the season, terrace talk of silverware to come was more of a famine than a feast, hence the delight of the Knowsley Road faithful when a veritable banquet was set before them. Youth, skill, speed and fitness lay at the heart of a success which saw Saints add to previous Championship triumphs of 1932, 1953 and 1959 and there were certain similarities to that latter game against Hunslet – not least the flair and fluency of Saints' handling.

Post-match press coverage suggested that Saints had 'nowt to beat' in dispatching a pedestrian and un-imaginative Thrum Hall outfit, but such a contention was unfair to Championship-seeking Saints, who were fully aware that history was within their grasp. This momentous victory was gained without ace South African winger Tom Van Vollenhoven, who was unfit. However, his deputy Tony Barrow – the brother of full-back Frank – came up trumps with a fine all-round display and he features amongst Saints' try-scorers. Points-wise, Saints hero was their other South African winger Len Killeen, who finished with 21 via a hat-trick of tries and six goals, while prop Albert Halsall was a revelation by crossing the Halifax line on three occasions to earn the Harry Sunderland trophy. There was no early indication of a drubbing to come for Halifax, who included former Saints hooker David Harrison in their line-up. Barry Cooper had opened the scoring with a penalty goal and, after Killeen had touched down for Saints, Terry Fogerty plunged over and Cooper converted to give the Yorkshire team a 7-3 lead. Halsall then opened his account before a Murphy drop-goal gave Saints an 8-7 advantage with half an hour gone. That lit the fuse for what proved to be a 29-point scoring spree by Saints, which included a further try by Halsall and two goals from Len Killeen, which allowed Saints a 15-7 cushion at half-time. Halsall completed his hat-trick on the restart and the barnstorming Albert was followed over the 'Fax line by Tony Barrow, before two typical individual efforts and a further four goals by Killeen made 28 May 1966 a real red-letter day for the Saints.

Despite exchanges being fast and furious throughout, the only 'incident' came when respective wingers Johnny Freeman (Halifax) and Tony Barrow (Saints) had a difference of opinion. This triggered an unseemly brawl involving most of the players and umbrella-wielding Saints supporter Minnie Cotton. Order was quickly restored by referee Joe Manley and the police, while the over-zealous female fan was escorted from the Station Road enclosure. Scrum-half Gordon Baker snatched a last-gasp consolation try for Halifax, to which Cooper tacked on his third goal while. From the Saints' perspective, Cumbrian-born Coach Joe Coan could be well satisfied with his first full season in the 'hot seat'.

Half time: 15-7

Harry Sunderland Trophy: A. Halsall (St Helens)

St Helens 35
Tries: Halsall (3), Killeen (3), A. Barrow
Goals: Killeen (6)
Drop goal: Murphy

Halifax 12
Tries: Fogerty, Baker
Goals: Cooper (3)

St Helens v. Halifax

Saints at the double! The team celebrate in the dressing room at Station Road after the thrashing of Halifax. Three-try hero Albert Halsall is second from the right, while full-back Frank Barrow (third from the left) shows the scars of battle! Notice the crate of Greenall's 'Champion' Ale in front of the trophy – a most appropriate celebration beverage!

St Helens: F. Barrow; A. Barrow, A. Murphy (captain), W. Benyon, L. Killeen; P. Harvey, T. Bishop; A. Halsall, W. Sayer, C. Watson, R. French, J. Warlow, J. Mantle.
Subs: R. Prosser, G. Hitchen.

Halifax: B. Cooper; D. Jones, J. Burnett (captain), C. Dixon, J. Freeman; B. Robinson, G. Baker; K. Roberts, D. Harrison, J. Scroby, T. Fogerty, T. Ramshaw, C. Renilson.
Subs: R. Eastwood, H. Duffy.

St Helens v. Leeds Championship final

16 May 1970
Odsal Stadium, Bradford

Attendance: 26,358
Referee: Mr Thompson (Huddersfield)

Saints' Coach Cliff Evans caused a sensation when he left leading scorer Frank Wilson out of the squad to face reigning champions Leeds at Odsal. Eric Prescott, a young second-row forward was the surprise choice to snuff out the threat posed by Leeds's right winger Alan Smith. The wisdom of the change was questioned after just 7 minutes, however, when Smith took a long pass and scorched in for the opening try. In what was already developing into a classic encounter, the Saints' response was quick and devastating. A well-rehearsed tap penalty move 30 yards from the Leeds line saw Mantle smash into the heart of the enemy defence before feeding Eric Chisnall. The big second-rower charged down the middle, drew the cover and passed one-handed to Frank Myler, who sent veteran hooker Bill Sayer under the posts.

Although the conversion put the Saints 5-3 in front, continual Leeds pressure forced Coslett to drop out from under his own cross-bar. His 40-yard effort was caught by Leeds' Scottish centre Ron Cowan, who embarked upon an incredible side-stepping run that carried him past seven bemused St Helens defenders to dive over near the posts for a wonderful solo try, leaving full-back John Holmes the simple task of adding the two points. Such a setback would surely have meant disaster for a lesser team, and Leeds, with stand-off Shoebottom in brilliant form, tried everything to increase their lead before half time. However, the Saints' defence remained rock-solid, bolstered by Coslett's 23rd minute penalty which kept them in contention at 7-8.

The turning point of the match came five minutes after the interval, as John Walsh popped over a crucial 25-yard drop-goal, to edge his team-mates ahead by a single point. It was the signal for the almighty St Helens pack to take control. Powerful runs from Chisnall, Watson and Mantle – who was suffering from a painful sprung shoulder – kept Leeds on the rack until another dazzling try in the 51st minute began the Saints' victory march. Six players joined in the movement before Myler's exquisitely timed reverse pass sent young Prescott racing away to touch down near the posts with a spectacular dive. Coslett's conversion hit the post, but Walsh made amends with his second drop-goal and as the storm clouds gathered menacingly overhead, the tenacious centre powered his way over for the try that effectively ended Leeds' championship hopes. A torrential downpour signalled the Loiners' demise, which sent fans scurrying for cover at both ends of the huge Odsal bowl – not that there was much! Yet Coslett ignored the atrocious conditions to increase the margin to 21-10 with two well-taken penalties. The pre-match favourites received a further jolt with five minutes to go when Eric Prescott, who had fully justified his controversial selection, picked up a loose pass intended for Smith and bounded over for his second try.

A battle-weary Cliff Watson proudly accepted the Championship Trophy from Lord Derby and held it aloft in an unashamed gesture of triumph. Frank Myler, who, like Watson, was soon to depart for the Australian tour, won the first championship medal of his long career and crowned a fabulous display with the Harry Sunderland Trophy as the outstanding player of the match.

Half time: 7-8

Harry Sunderland Trophy: F. Myler (St Helens)

St Helens 24
Tries: Prescott (2), Walsh, Sayer
Goals: Coslett (4)
Drop goals: Walsh (2)

Leeds 12
Tries: Cowan, Smith
Goals: Holmes (3)

St Helens v. Leeds

Below: Saints full-back Frankie Barrow saves at the feet of Leeds centre Syd Hynes, assisted by 'emergency' winger Eric Prescott.

St Helens: F. Barrow; L. Jones, W. Benyon, J. Walsh, E. Prescott; F. Myler, J. Heaton; A. Halsall, W. Sayer, C. Watson (captain), J. Mantle, E. Chisnall, K. Coslett.
Subs: A. Whittle, G. Rees.

Leeds: J. Holmes; A. Smith, S. Hynes, R. Cowan, J. Atkinson; M. Shoebottom, B. Seabourne (captain); J. Burke, A. Crosby, A. Eyre, W. Ramsey, G. Eccles, R. Batten.
Subs: D. Hick, J. Langley.

St Helens v. Wigan Floodlit Trophy semi-final (replay)

13 December 1970
Knowsley Road, St Helens

Attendance: 18,453
Referee: Mr Lawrinson (Warrington)

The 1970/71 season saw Saints and Wigan go head-to-head no less than six times in three competitions. Wigan were league leaders at the end of the campaign, winning 30 out of 34 matches. Although the Cherry and Whites won at Knowsley Road on Boxing Day, the Saints gained revenge with a 9-6 success on Good Friday. Yet it was in cup-tie football that the Saints held sway over the Old Enemy. They smashed Wigan 23-0 in the Lancashire Cup semi-final at Central Park in October and won a 'smash-and-grab' victory in the Championship final at Swinton courtesy of Billy Benyon's late touchdown.

In the Floodlit Trophy competition, the two sides had drawn 7-7 at Central Park and a replay was convened at Knowsley Road on 13 December – the first ever Sunday fixture at the famous old ground. Admission was by programme – apparently spectators could not be charged directly for admission on the Sabbath – and a healthy crowd approaching 19,000 assembled under a cloudless sky. They witnessed a gripping contest, which could have gone either way. Indeed, for three-quarters of the game, the two evenly matched teams vied for supremacy with a succession of penalties and drop-goals. Saints' skipper Kel Coslett and Wigan's Colin Tyrer were engaged in a penalty contest, while the two sides had match-winning drop-goal exponents in John Walsh and Wigan second-rower Bill Ashurst.

Well into the last quarter, it was the Saints who broke the defensive deadlock, when flying winger Les Jones notched a try from a move which began on half-way, with his centre partner Benyon's crucial break and kick-ahead an integral part. At 13-10 Saints had the advantage, yet Wigan stormed back with ten minutes to go when Welsh winger Keri Jones picked up a loose ball following Francis' kick and darted over to give Tyrer an easy conversion. Saints did not throw in the towel and Eric Chisnall punched a hole through Wigan's defence on his own 25 line and fed Benyon. He got Jones moving along the touchline and was there to take his inside pass and plunge over as the Wigan defenders made desperate attempts to cover the danger – it was a superb finish to the tightest of matches! It always seemed that Saints held a big advantage over Wigan – and most teams – with the dominance of Bill Benyon and John Walsh in the centres. Defensively solid, they were also able to provide wingers Wilson and Jones with innumerable running chances. What's more, they were 'home grown' to boot! Despite Benyon's heroics, the Saints went on to lose narrowly in the Floodlit Trophy final to a powerful Leeds side, enjoying home advantage at Headingley, just two days after this classic match at Knowsley Road. A victory would have been an unbelievable achievement in the circumstances.

Half time: 6-4

St Helens 16
Tries: Jones, Benyon
Goals: Coslett (3)
Drop goal: Walsh

Wigan 15
Try: K. Jones
Goals: Tyrer (4)
Drop goals: Ashurst (2)

ST HELENS v. WIGAN

The Saints' line up before the 1971 Championship final against Wigan at Station Road Swinton, another tightly fought cup tie in the tradition of previous 'derby' clashes! From left to right, back row: Tony Karalius (hooker), Bob Blackwood (left wing), Jon Stephens (front row), Eric Chisnall (second row), John Mantle (second row), Graham Rees (front row), Bob Wanbon (substitute forward), John Walsh (centre). Front row: Ken Kelly (substitute back), Alan Whittle (stand-off), Jeff Heaton (scrum-half), Kel Coslett (captain and loose forward), Geoff Pimblett (full-back), Les Jones (right wing), Billy Benyon (centre).

ST. HELENS RUGBY FOOTBALL CLUB LTD.
B.B.C. 2 FLOODLIT TROPHY—SEMI-FINAL REPLAY

ST. HELENS v. WIGAN

AT KNOWSLEY ROAD, ST. HELENS
ON SUNDAY, 13th DECEMBER, 1970
KICK-OFF 2.30 p.m.

TEAMS

ST. HELENS	WIGAN
Colours: Royal Blue Jerseys, White Shorts	Colours: Cherry & White Hoops, White Shorts
Fullback	**Fullback**
1. BARROW, F.	1. TYRER, C.
Threequarters	**Threequarters**
2. JONES, L.	2. JONES, K.
3. BENYON, W.	3. AYRES, W.
4. WALSH, J.	4. FRANCIS, W.
5. WILSON, F.	5. WRIGHT, S.
Halfbacks	**Halfbacks**
6. WHITTLE, A.	6. HILL, D.
7. HEATON, J.	7. PARR, F.
Forwards	**Forwards**
8. HALSALL, A.	8. HOGAN, B.
9. KARALIUS, A.	9. CLARKE, C.
10. CHISNALL, E.	10. FLETCHER, G.
11. MANTLE, J.	11. ASHURST, W.
12. PRESCOTT, E.	12. ROBINSON, D.
13. COSLETT, T. K.	13. LAUGHTON, D.
Substitutes from	Substitutes
14. MYLER, F.	14. O'LOUGHLIN, K.
15. GLOVER, B.	15. CUNNINGHAM, E.
REES, G.	

Referee: Mr. E. LAWRINSON (Warrington)
Touch Judges: Mr. F. BESWICK, Mr. R. WELSBY

ADMISSION INCLUDING PROGRAMME 6/-

St Helens: F. Barrow; L. Jones, W. Benyon, J. Walsh, F. Wilson; A. Whittle, J. Heaton; A. Halsall, A. Karalius, E. Chisnall, J. Mantle, E. Prescott, K. Coslett (captain).
Subs: F. Myler, G. Rees.

Wigan: C. Tyrer; K. Jones, W. Francis, Kevin O'Loughlin, S. Wright; D. Hill, F. Parr; B. Hogan, R. Burdell, G. Fletcher, W. Ashurst, D. Robinson, D. Laughton (captain).
Subs: Kieron O'Loughlin, E. Cunningham.

St Helens v. Wigan Championship final

22 May 1971
Station Road, Swinton

Attendance: 21,743
Referee: Mr Lawrinson (Warrington)

The first-ever Championship final clash between St Helens and Wigan provided a magnificent spectacle. This game of fast, open rugby provided BBC commentator Eddie Waring and millions of television viewers with one of the most exciting grandstand finishes of them all – certainly not without controversy! As expected, the game began at a cracking pace, with all the intensity of a typical 'derby' cup-tie. The Riversiders' only tangible reward for their early dominance was a 9th minute try from the former Swinton forward Dave Robinson as St Helens skipper Kel Coslett booted over two penalties and a drop-goal to give his side a 6-3 advantage at half time.

Second-rower Bill Ashurst, whose tactical kicking had already caused problems for the Saints' defence, scored a superb diving try shortly after the restart to give the Cherry and Whites a crucial two-point lead. The title seemed to be heading for Central Park, especially after John Mantle was dismissed by referee Lawrinson for retaliation. Indeed, two towering drop-goals from man of the match Ashurst put Wigan firmly in control at 12-6 as the St Helens 'twelve' mounted a desperate bid for victory with just seven minutes remaining.

The never-say-die Saints swept the ball from right flank to left, creating the perfect overlap for Cumbrian winger Bob Blackwood to scamper over in the corner. A magnificent touchline conversion from a seemingly ice-cool Coslett – one of the most important kicks of his distinguished career - put his team-mates into contention at 11-12 and set up the most sensational climax in Championship final history! Some incredible close-support play saw the Saints surge into the Wigan half before losing possession with the line in sight. Rather than consolidate, Ashurst and former Saint Doug Laughton combined to send Kevin O'Loughlin away on the right. The winger tried to find Dave Hill with an inside pass, but, somewhat alarmingly for Wigan, the ball went to ground to give St Helens one last chance of saving the game. As the seconds ticked away, John Walsh sliced a drop-goal attempt from 40 yards, which flashed high and wide to the right of the Wigan posts – with centre Billy Benyon following up at a tremendous pace! Disregarding the pain from his injured

Half time: 6-3

Harry Sunderland Trophy: W. Ashurst (Wigan)

St Helens 16
Tries: Blackwood, Benyon
Goals: Coslett (4)
Drop goal: Coslett

Wigan 12
Tries: Robinson, Ashurst
Goal: Tyrer
Drop goals: Ashurst (2)

St Helens v. Wigan

Centre Billy Benyon, Saints' very own 'One-armed Bandit' plunges over the line to give his team an unlikely victory over deadly rivals Wigan. Opposing winger Stuart Wright is powerless to prevent the three points. Benyon's record of consistency is remarkable. He is one of only three St Helens-born players to have chalked up over 500 appearances for the club during their careers – Eric Chisnall and William Briers are the other two – with Welshman Kel Coslett also achieving this incredible milestone.

right shoulder, which he had 'carried' for over an hour of the match, Benyon caught the ball on the bounce and threw himself over the line with Wigan winger Stuart Wright powerless to stop him. Although Wigan players were indignant that he was offside, referee Lawrinson had no hesitation in awarding the touchdown. Clearly in some distress from his injury, Benyon was replaced by Ken Kelly, but it was only a token gesture as the referee blew for full-time after another superbly-judged Coslett conversion. The 'One-Armed Bandit' had turned what looked like a certain Wigan victory into an unbelievable 16-12 Saints' success and, following on from the previous season, a memorable Championship 'double' celebration into the bargain. Yet the arguments about the validity of Benyon's last-gasp try raged long after Lord Pilkington had presented the trophy to Captain Coslett. 'I've always maintained I was onside,' Benyon insisted, 'and the record books bear me out!'

St Helens: G. Pimblett; L. Jones, W. Benyon, J. Walsh, R. Blackwood; A. Whittle, J. Heaton; J. Stephens, A. Karalius, G. Rees, J. Mantle, E. Chisnall, K. Coslett (captain).
Subs: K. Kelly, R. Wanbon.

Wigan: C. Tyrer; K. O'Loughlin, W. Francis, P. Rowe, S. Wright; D. Hill, W. Ayres; B. Hogan, C. Clarke, G. Fletcher, W. Ashurst, D. Robinson, D. Laughton (captain).
Subs: E. Cunningham, D. Gandy.

St Helens v. Leeds Challenge Cup final

13 May 1972
Wembley Stadium, London

Attendance: 89,495
Referee: Mr Lawrinson (Warrington)

Injury and goal-kicking proved to be significant factors in the destiny of the Challenge Cup when St Helens met major rivals Leeds in 1971/72. Saints' forwards Eric Prescott and Tony Karalius were already ruled out; John Mantle had to play with twelve stitches in his head after a car accident and Stephens, Chisnall and Heaton were all carrying minor knocks. Full-back John Holmes was Leeds' only real doubt, passing a fitness test on his injured ankle a few hours before the start – a decision which had a considerable bearing on the final result. Almost 90,000 fans saw Kel Coslett kick off deep into the Leeds half, almost two minutes before the appointed three o'clock starting time. After the third tackle, with the Loiners penned in their own twenty-five, acting half-back Tony Fisher threw the ball back for the customary clearance kick – with disastrous results. Cookson and Clarkson had both called for the pass and the ball rolled loose, forcing a desperate Keith Hepworth to try and clear his lines. His effort was charged down by the fast-moving Saints' veteran Graham Rees, who calmly picked up and plunged over for a vital touchdown in just 35 seconds, making it Wembley's fastest ever try! The plan to 'shield' normal kicker Holmes by sharing the duties between Cookson and Clawson had backfired dramatically as Coslett's measured conversion gave the Saints' morale an even bigger boost!

Such an early setback, coupled with some solid St Helens defence clearly unnerved the Yorkshiremen. Clawson's failure from two kickable penalties mirrored Leeds' uncertainty, although he registered his side's first points in the 11th minute after Coslett had dropped out on the full. Yet five minutes later, Leeds lost the ball deep in their own half once again. Heaton began a sweeping cross-field move which saw Eric Chisnall scatter two defenders on a powerful run down the right with all the Leeds cover drawn inside to try and cover the danger. Chisnall's brilliant long pass was gleefully accepted by Les Jones, who scampered in at the corner with opposite number Atkinson out of position and unable to recover!

Coslett's attempted conversion shaved the left-hand post, but a magnificent penalty goal just inside his own half in the 22nd minute gave St Helens a 10-2 lead as the terraces echoed to the strains of 'When the Saints Go Marching In'. Leeds faced an enormous challenge and while Clawson pulled four points back with two penalties, Coslett responded with another special from half-way for a 12-6 interval scoreline.

Coach Jim Challinor talked about containment for the first ten minutes of the second half. Yet after just sixty seconds the powerful Cookson burst through to touch down under the posts. To the utter disbelief of Leeds and their supporters, however, Clawson missed the chance to cut the lead to one point by stabbing the ball low and wide of the target – a moment reminiscent of Wakefield's Don Fox in 1968 and almost as crucial! As the drizzle turned into a downpour, Coslett, the kicker supreme, piled on the agony with penalty number four and he later unleashed a huge 30 yard drop-goal which soared fully ten feet above the uprights as another Leeds revival looked imminent. Two further Clawson penalties reduced the deficit to 16-13 and for Kel Coslett the tension was beginning to tell: 'We got the message from the bench…10 minutes to go! It was a great relief and I felt that we were playing well enough to hold them until full-time.' The sheer ferocity of the St Helens' tackling saw to that and the Challenge Cup remained in Lancashire for the second successive year at Leeds' expense.

Half time: 12-6

Lance Todd Trophy: K. Coslett (St Helens)

St Helens 16
Tries: Rees, Jones
Goals: Coslett (4)
Drop goal: Coslett

Leeds 13
Try: Cookson
Goals: Clawson (5)

St Helens v. Leeds

The prelude to Saints' second try, as second-rower Eric Chisnall scatters the cover, ready to fire the perfect cut-out pass to winger Les Jones, who went in at the corner. Leeds' winger John Atkinson races back desperately to cover out wide, but to no avail!

St Helens: G. Pimblett; L. Jones, W. Benyon, J. Walsh, F. Wilson; K. Kelly, J. Heaton; G. Rees, L. Greenall, J. Stephens, J. Mantle, E. Chisnall, K. Coslett (captain).
Subs: A. Whittle, K. Earl.

Leeds: J. Holmes; A. Smith, S. Hynes, L. Dyl, J. Atkinson; A. Hardisty (captain), K. Hepworth; T. Clawson, T. Fisher, W. Ramsey, P. Cookson, R. Haigh, R. Batten.
Subs: J. Langley, D. Ward.

St Helens v. Leeds

Saints stand-off Ken Kelly gets another attack moving in the 1972 final. Scrum-half Jeff Heaton is behind him. Kelly did much to subdue the danger of his opposite number, Alan Hardisty, which was one of the main reasons for his team's success.

Two Wembley cup winners – and try-scorers – celebrate their induction into the St Helens Past Players Hall of Fame in 1998. Les Jones (1972 and 1976) shares the spotlight with Frank Carlton, who scored the crucial opening try in the 1956 final against Halifax – the first time that the Saints had tasted success at Wembley.

St Helens v. Leeds

The *Sunday Mirror* produced a special sports supplement in the early 1970s. The edition of 14 May 1972 featured the contrasting fortunes of two teams: St Helens RLFC, who had beaten Leeds in a marvellous match at Wembley and the England soccer team, who had played out a dismal 0-0 draw with West Germany in Berlin and faced elimination from the European Nations Cup, costing manager Alf Ramsey his job. The thousands of soccer fans who had switched over to Independent Television for soccer coverage after watching the first half of the rugby league on the BBC probably wished they had not bothered – they had missed a real classic!

St Helens v. Widnes Challenge Cup final

8 May 1976
Wembley Stadium, London

Attendance: 90,000
Referee: Mr R. Moore (Wakefield)

Battle honours all round was the order of the day after 'old campaigners' Saints earned a superb tactical victory in this compelling derby clash in the metropolis. Fielding several players over thirty, Saints were dismissed by the media as 'Dad's Army' in tackling a youthful Widnes squad, also having physical superiority and included eleven of the side which lifted the trophy against Warrington in 1975. But it was the long in the tooth Saints who lasted the pace better in soaring temperatures, while coach Eric Ashton's master plan of first stifling the Chemics' ponderous pack before counter-attacking in the last quarter paid rich dividends.

However, the issue hung in the balance until the 68th minute with Saints clinging to a tenuous 7-5 lead. Then a try by Jeff Heaton allowed a little breathing space prior to a late points surge which sealed the Saints' fifth-successive Challenge Cup win. This came via substitute Peter Glynn – ironically a Widnesian – who became the first Saint to score two tries in a Wembley showdown. He might not have had the chance but for being preferred to Frank Wilson at the eleventh hour. Captain Kel Coslett marshalled his troops admirably for this final assault on the Chemics' fortress, while five-goal full-back Geoff Pimblett proved an able lieutenant in winning the Lance Todd Trophy on an energy-sapping afternoon, when all fifteen Saints were worthy of consideration.

The key to Saints' success was epitomized by veteran Welsh prop John Mantle, who covered every inch of the hallowed Wembley turf in his quest for a third winner's medal. Incidentally, the versatile Mantle appeared at loose forward versus Wigan in 1966 and then in the second-row against Leeds in 1972. Jubilant John said later: 'We were like marathon runners even though some of the Saints were on the wrong side of thirty. We kept going in searing heat that left us dehydrated and needing salt tablets and cold baths after the game. But Saints were all over Widnes in the last twenty minutes and that was crucial.'

Saints had fought their way to a seventh Wembley appearance with victories over Hull, Salford and Oldham, before earning the right for a trip to London with a nail-biting 5-4 win against Keighley at Fartown, Huddersfield, when Heaton was the try-scoring hero. A further point of interest for the 1976 blockbuster against Widnes was that the former Aberavon full-back Coslett handed the goal-kicking role to Geoff Pimblett, even though Kel was Saints' record holder with 1,639. 'There was a simple explanation,' said Geoff, 'because I had been kicking them all season after Kel had been injured. But he did have one attempt at Wembley.'

Led into the arena by chairman Charlie Martin, Saints took the lead with a 12th minute try by Eddie Cunningham (the brother of Kieron). A brilliant break by Billy Benyon created Eddie's chance and Pimblett added the conversion. Widnes hit back with a penalty by full-back Ray Dutton before Pimblett's snap drop-goal increased Saints' margin to 6-2, but the Knowsley Road team swapped ends just two points in front after Dutton found the target once more. The tit for tat scoring pattern was maintained on the restart, when Widnes hooker Keith 'Chiefy' Elwell landed a drop-goal and Pimblett quickly followed suit with his second one-pointer. An almost hour-long try impasse was finally ended when Pimblett, Derek Noonan and Tony Karalius engineered Heaton's game-breaking touchdown, and Pimblett again tacked on the extra points.

Half time: 6-4

Lance Todd Trophy: G. Pimblett (St Helens)

St Helens 20
Tries: Glynn (2), Heaton, Cunningham
Goals: Pimblett (3)
Drop goals: Pimblett (2)

Widnes 5
Goals: Dutton (2)
Drop goal: Elwell

St Helens v. Widnes

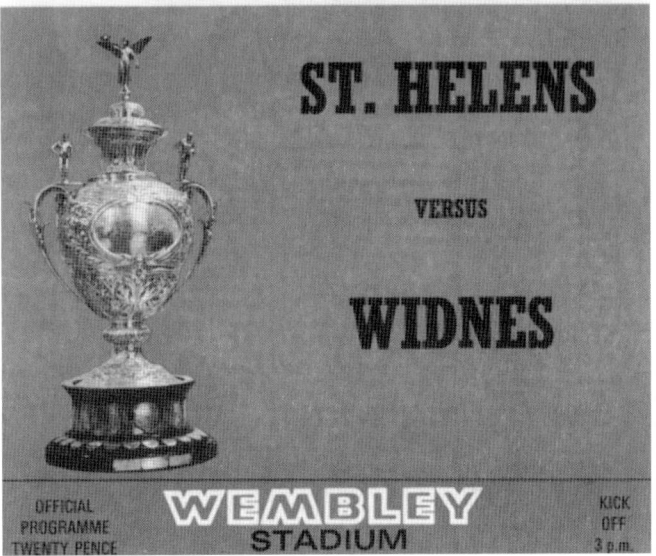

Enter super-sub Glynn to fire the final salvo, with his first try – the fruits of dextrous handling by Karalius – and his second the result of a kick-and-chase over the Widnes line. So it was a proud, if exhausted, Coslett who received the Challenge Cup from the leader of the opposition, Margaret Thatcher, at Wembley in 1976, while the customary hero's welcome awaited Saints on returning to St Helens. On an individual note, Saints fielded eight locals in their ranks, all of whom still lived in the Glass Town in 2002. They are Pimblett, Jones, Cunningham, Noonan, Benyon, Heaton, Chisnall, and Hull. But the Widnes-born representation was even greater, with only Prescott, Jenkins and Eckersley the odd men out of the fifteen. How times have changed!

St Helens: G. Pimblett; L. Jones, E. Cunningham, D. Noonan, R. Mathias; W. Benyon, J. Heaton; J. Mantle, A. Karalius, K. Coslett (*captain*), G. Nicholls, E. Chisnall, D. Hull.
Subs: P. Glynn, M. James.

Widnes: R. Dutton; A. Prescott, E. Hughes, M. George, D. Jenkins; D. Eckersley, R. Bowden (*captain*); M. Nelson, K. Elwell, J. Wood, J. Foran, M. Adams, D. Laughton.
Subs: D. O'Neill, B. Sheridan.

St Helens v. Widnes

Key moments and personalities from a classic Cup Final. *Above:* Eddie Cunningham scores Saints' crucial first try from a Billy Benyon break, to the delight of the travelling Red and White Army. *Below:* 'Supersub' Peter Glynn, who scored a brace of touchdowns to bring the cup back to Knowsley Road, takes on the Widnes defence in the shape of Mick George (left) and former Saint Dave Eckersley. John Mantle is the other St Helens player in the photograph.

ST HELENS v. WIDNES

Above: Agony and ecstasy! Delight on the Saints bench, as Jeff Heaton scores a crucial second-half try. Coach Eric Ashton (bottom left) sits impassively. Players behind him are Mel James (substitute forward), reserves Harry Pinner and Graham Liptrot, with injured stand-off Billy Benyon, who had been replaced by Peter Glynn.
Below: Coach Eric Ashton (left) and skipper Kel Coslett enjoy the fruits of success. One of the warmest cup finals on record had clearly taken its toll on the Saints captain!

St Helens v. Leeds Challenge Cup final

13 May 1978
Wembley Stadium, London

Attendance: 95,872
Referee: Mr W. Thompson (Huddersfield)

In what was billed as the Queen's Jubilee Cup Final, Saints' skipper Geoff Pimblett kicked deep into the Leeds half to begin the traditionally fierce opening exchanges. After just four minutes, young loose forward Harry Pinner unleashed a towering 'bomb' which drifted tantalizingly towards the Leeds try-line. Full-back Oulton's attempted catch saw the ball bounce off his arms and rebound off fellow defender Atkinson. Saints' young hooker Graham Liptrot, following up speedily, latched onto the loose ball and touched down for a splendid try which Pimblett converted with ease – it was a fantastic start, reminiscent of Graham Rees's vital charge-down try in 1972. The beleaguered Leeds defence was given but a temporary reprieve in the 13th minute, when referee Thompson ordered a scrum after Nicholls lost possession five yards from the line. A magnificent heel by Graham Liptrot from the Leeds 'put-in' brought scrum-half Gwilliam into action with a well-timed pass to Bill Francis. Two dazzling sidesteps left bemused Leeds tacklers clutching thin air as the classy stand off strode in for a try near the posts. A thunderous roar greeted Pimblett's second goal which opened up a ten-point gap. No team had ever recovered from such a deficit in a Challenge Cup final. Yet as the game went on, there were ominous signs that perhaps the Saints had peaked too soon! Leeds began to claw themselves back into contention in the 22rd minute when Atkinson took a suspiciously forward pass from Dyl and ran 30 yards for the Yorkshire side's first try. Although Oulton added a splendid touchline conversion, Geoff Pimblett's 34th minute penalty ensured that the Saints went in at half time with a comfortable 12-5 lead.

During the interval, Leeds coach Syd Hynes gave his forwards strict instructions to drive down the middle and resist the temptation to open out play. Within a minute of the restart, the Loiners's heavier pack steamrollered up to the St Helens 25, where skipper David Ward dropped a goal. This was a great psychological boost for his team-mates, who gradually began to take control with ace schemer John Holmes a constant threat. In what was always going to be a riveting encounter, Holmes was the architect of Leeds' second try after 55 minutes, when winger David Smith touched down in the corner to reduce the deficit to 12-9. The timely introduction of substitutes Kevin Dick and prop Roy Dickinson gave Leeds added impetus in the last quarter, as second-rower Cookson crashed through three St Helens defenders to level the scores at 12-12. Oulton missed the conversion, but as tension reached fever pitch in the 75th minute, John Holmes's snap drop-goal at the end of another forward surge put Leeds ahead for the first time. Three minutes later, Ward dropped his second goal for a further bit of breathing space at 14-12 – but there was more drama to come!

In one of the most sensational finishes in Cup Final history, the Saints mounted a last desperate attack to try and save the match. The attempt ended in tragedy, however, when Derek Noonan failed to hold a pass from his co-centre Peter Glynn, with the line seemingly at his mercy. As the Leeds players celebrated their second successive Challenge Cup final victory, Derek Noonan reflected ruefully on what might have been. 'If I'd caught the ball, I was in,' he maintains. 'I picked my spot, there was no-one in front of me and I think I only had three yards to go. Shoulder down, I was pretty sure I'd have gone in!' Leeds' superior forward power, coupled with the immaculate form of stand-off John Holmes, had won the day. Yet it was a Saint who won the coveted man of the match award. George Nicholls was an outstanding candidate throughout, with a devastating display of powerhouse running and tackling.

Half time: 12-5

Lance Todd Trophy: G. Nicholls (St Helens)

St Helens 12
Tries: Liptrot, Francis
Goals: Pimblett (3)

Leeds 14
Tries: Atkinson, D. Smith, Cookson
Goal: Oulton
Drop goals: Ward (2), Holmes

St Helens v. Leeds

The beginning of the end! Leeds stand-off John Holmes drops a vital goal to give his team the lead late in the second half, despite the efforts of Bill Francis (left) and skipper Geoff Pimblett.

St Helens: G. Pimblett (*captain*); L. Jones, D. Noonan, P. Glynn, R. Mathias; W. Francis, K. Gwilliam; D. Chisnall, G. Liptrot, M. James, G. Nicholls, E. Cunningham, H. Pinner.
Subs: A. Ashton, A. Karalius.

Leeds: W. Oulton; D. Smith, N. Hague, L. Dyl, J. Atkinson; J. Holmes, S. Sanderson; M. Harrison, D. Ward (*captain*), S. Pitchford, G. Eccles, P. Cookson, M. Crane.
Subs: K. Dick, R. Dickinson.

St Helens v. Wigan Lancashire Cup final

26 October 1984
Central Park, Wigan

Attendance: 26,074
Referee: Mr R. Campbell (Widnes)

The Saints were riding high on the adrenalin of the arrival of Australian superstar Mal Meninga during the early part of the 1984/85 campaign. The mouth-watering prospect of a Lancashire Cup final clash with deadly rivals Wigan was originally earmarked for Warrington's Wilderspool Stadium. Such was the interest, however, that both finalists protested that a 16,000-capacity stadium was too small for the massive support anticipated. Wigan won the toss to play the match at Central Park – the first time that a final had not been held at a neutral venue and it was the first to be played on a Sunday afternoon.

The 26,074 spectators who packed the terraces on that murky October afternoon witnessed a devastating first-half performance of awesome power and ball-handling skill as Meninga ruthlessly exposed the defensive frailties of Wigan's right flank. The 15st giant took less than seven minutes to make his presence felt. Taking hooker Graham Liptrot's pass about fifteen yards from the line, he sold a brilliant dummy to John Ferguson, before bulldozing his way over for Saints' opening try.

St Helens continued to dominate and skipper Harry Pinner began another fine move with a superb pass for Andy Platt to pierce the Riversiders' defence. He handed on to fellow second-rower Paul Round, who was halted inches from the line by a last-ditch Ferguson tackle. Meninga, at acting half back, almost casually fed the eager Roy Haggerty, an early replacement for the injured Phil Veivers, who charged in from close range. The conversion put St Helens 12-2 ahead and in the 35th minute the ball was swept, inevitably, over to the left once again after Graeme West had lost possession. Neil Holding fed Meninga on the burst and although three Wigan defenders tried to contain him, Big Mal still managed to conjure up the perfect ball for winger Sean Day to score in the corner. A minute before half time, the strong-running Round looped over a one-handed pass to Mighty Mal in full cry. He handed off fellow Aussie Mark Cannon with contemptuous ease, leaving full-back Sean Edwards with the hopeless task of preventing yet more Meninga mayhem!

Despite the shock of a seemingly unassailable 24-2 deficit, Wigan took the game to St Helens after the interval and produced a splendid fight-back, with tries from winger Henderson Gill, skipper Graeme West and Nicky Kiss, with centre Whitfield adding two goals. Just when the game seemed delicately poised, however, Meninga was inexplicably singled out for some special attention by two Wigan forwards as he ran the ball up to the home twenty-five – a fit of pique doubtless born out of sheer frustration! Super-cool Sean Day's penalty goal eased the visitors' jangling nerves and clinched a 26-18 victory for the Saints, their first major trophy success for seven years.

Half time: 24-2

St Helens 26
Tries: Meninga (2), Haggerty, Day
Goals: Day (5)

Wigan 18
Tries: Gill, Kiss
Goals: Whitfield (3)

St Helens v. Wigan

St Helens RLFC Lancashire Cup Winners 1984. From left to right, back row: Phil Veivers, Paul Round, Peter Gorley, Mal Meninga, Roy Haggerty, Andy Platt. Middle row: Eric Leach (Kit), Graham Liptrot, Harry Pinner (captain), Tony Burke, Steve Peters, Shaun Allen. Front row: Denis Litherland, Sean Day, Neil Holding, Barrie Ledger.

St Helens: P. Veivers; B. Ledger, S. Allen, M. Meninga, S. Day; C. Arkwright, N. Holding; A. Burke, G. Liptrot, P. Gorley, A. Platt, P. Round, H. Pinner (*captain*).
Subs: J. Smith, R. Haggerty.

Wigan: S. Edwards; J. Ferguson, D. Stephenson, C. Whitfield, H. Gill; M. Cannon, J. Fairhurst; N. Courtney, N. Kiss, B. Case, G. West (captain), S. Wane, I. Potter.
Subs: J. Pendlebury, M. Scott.

St Helens v. Hull Kingston Rovers Premiership final

11 May 1985
Elland Road, Leeds

Attendance: 15,518
Referee: Mr Wall (Leigh)

Hull Kingston Rovers had dented the Saints' ambitions of top honours in the 1984/85 campaign, pipping them to the First Division championship by three points and dumping them unceremoniously out of the Challenge Cup at Knowsley Road. There was a chance for revenge, however, as the two sides clashed in the Premiership Final at Elland Road, Leeds, with Rovers seeking their second successive League and Premiership 'double'. Yet on their day, the Saints, led by ace loose forward Harry Pinner, could hold their own with anyone. Indeed, it took just two minutes for the St Helens attacking machine to swing into action. An astute ball from Pinner sent prop Peter Gorley surging through the Rovers' defence before handing on to Chris Arkwright, whose inside pass left hooker Gary Ainsworth with a 25-yard dash to the posts. Sean Day's conversion was a formality.

Although Rovers levelled the scores with a try and goal from Fairbairn, the Saints responded with another devastating piece of support play. Second-rower Roy Haggerty did the initial spadework, before feeding Barrie Ledger with a clever one-handed pass. Full-back Phil Veivers, backing up on the inside, finished the move in style!

Halfway through an entertaining first period, it was time for giant Australian centre Mal Meninga to make his presence felt. Mighty Mal latched onto a brilliant ball from Holding and surged down the left touchline, before being felled just short of the Rovers twenty-five by a near-suicidal Fairbairn crash-tackle. Quick hands by Holding, Platt, Pinner and Peters swept the ball across the field to create the perfect overlap for Barrie Ledger, whose searing pace did the rest. Hull KR soon reduced the deficit to 10-16 with a try from winger Laws. Stung out of their complacency, the St Helens defence pinned the Humbersiders in their own half with some dynamic tackling from young second-rower Andy Platt. In a desperate attempt to get his three-quarters moving, Rovers' loose forward Hall, a replacement for the injured Australian Gavin Miller, fired out a long wide pass straight into the hands of Meninga, who gratefully cruised to the line from 30 yards. Day's goal gave the cock-a-hoop Saints a 22-10 advantage. Yet as half time approached, Kiwi prop Mark Broadhurst crashed through to put centre Robinson in for an unconverted try.

Half time: 22-14

Harry Sunderland Trophy: H. Pinner (St Helens)

St Helens 36
Tries: Ledger (2), Meninga (2), Veivers, Ainsworth, Pinner
Goals: Day (4)

Hull Kingston Rovers 16
Tries: Fairbairn, Robinson, Laws
Goals: Fairbairn (2)

ST HELENS v. HULL KINGSTON ROVERS

Flying machine! Barrie Ledger touches down for his first try after some brilliant passing had created the overlap. Ian Robinson (left) and Gordon Smith of Hull KR are powerless to prevent the four-pointer!

The game was still in the melting pot after the interval, as the Saints, still to win a scrum, were forced to withstand a series of all-out assaults from a Rovers' side determined to gain the ascendancy. A Fairbairn penalty gave the Robins fresh impetus at 22-16, until the unfortunate Hall attempted another disastrous lofted pass. Meninga loomed large once again, to pluck the ball out of the air and showed incredible pace for such a big man by holding off speedster Gary Clark and George Fairbairn in an incredible 75-yard dash to the line! Mighty Mal's superb opportunism finally dispelled any chance of a 'Rover's Return' as the Saints finished like they had begun, with some classic running rugby league! In the 72nd minute, Harry Pinner crowned a stunning man of the match performance by waltzing past six bemused Hull KR defenders for the sixth St Helens try, which Day converted.

Virtually on the final hooter, another superbly timed Pinner pass sent Holding scorching to halfway before feeding Shaun Allen. Barrie Ledger gratefully accepted the substitute's overhead pass to clinch a Premiership record score of 36-16 and set the seal on a marvellous team performance and a truly classic encounter. Harry Pinner, whose leadership qualities and superb ball-handling skills had been so vital to the Saints' success, proudly accepted the Premiership Trophy on behalf of his team-mates after his 300th game for the club.

St Helens: P. Veivers; B. Ledger, S. Peters, M. Meninga, S. Day; C. Arkwright, N. Holding; A. Burke, G. Ainsworth, P. Gorley, A. Platt, R. Haggerty, H. Pinner (*captain*).
Subs: S. Allen, P. Forber.

Hull Kingston Rovers: G. Fairbairn; G. Clark, I. Robinson, G. Prohm, D. Laws; M. Smith, G. Smith; M. Broadhurst, D. Watkinson (*captain*), A. Ema, A. Kelly, P. Hogan, S. Hall.
Subs: P. Harkin, J. Lydiat.

St Helens v. Hull Kingston Rovers

Enduring images from a marvellous game of Rugby League! Livewire scrum-half Neil Holding (above) looks to off-load, despite the attentions of Hull KR second-rower Phil Hogan. The thrill of the chase (below) as Australian superstar Mal Meninga leaves Gary Clark and George Fairbairn in his wake as he scores his second try.

ST HELENS v. HULL KINGSTON ROVERS

Harry Pinner's Heroes! The Super Saints celebrate on the Elland Road pitch after a marvellous climax to the 1984/85 campaign. From left to right, back row: Front-rower Tony Burke, a model of consistency; Cumbrian forward Peter Gorley, as tough as granite; Barrie Ledger, Saints' leading scorer during the campaign with 30 touchdowns; Paul Forber, full of youthful exuberance and a Saint for many years to come; Harry Pinner, the best loose forward in the game in the mid 1980s; Andy Platt, hard-running and tackling second-rower; Gary Ainsworth, on-loan hooker from Leigh, but what a signing; Phil Veivers (hidden), Australian full-back par excellence; Sean Day, the League's leading goalkicker in 1884/85 with 157; Australian superstar Mal Meninga, one of the world's greatest-ever centres. Front row: Steve Peters, tough half-back or centre; Neil Holding, scrum-half with lightening turn of pace; Shaun Allen, a local lad who could play in the centre or at loose forward.

St Helens v. Halifax Challenge Cup final

2 May 1987
Wembley Stadium, London

Attendance: 91,267
Referee: Mr Holdsworth (Kippax)

The Saints of 1986/87 were famed for their 'off-the-cuff' style of attacking football. Unfortunately, rivals Wigan, with a more disciplined approach, had won everything except the coveted Challenge Cup! Needless to say, coach Alex Murphy and his men had their eyes on Wembley glory. The younger St Helens side had power and mobility in all areas of the field. At full-back Australian Phil Veivers could join the attack with devastating effect. In the three-quarters there was the pace and power of centres Paul Loughlin and long-striding Kiwi Mark Elia. Outside them, Barrie Ledger and Kevin McCormack were real flyers. Livewire half-backs Neil Holding and Australian stand-off Brett Clark could be a real handful on their day and in the pack, the back three of Andy Platt, Roy Haggerty and skipper Chris Arkwright were as potent a force as any on their day. If anything was missing, however, it was experience. In so many Wembley finals, the ability to keep a cool head has had such an important part to play. This was certainly one of the factors in 1987, as the daunting atmosphere caused the young Saints to 'freeze', especially in the early stages, as the team squandered several clear scoring chances through careless handling. Halifax, inspired by the mighty presence of veteran Australian full-back Graham Eadie, went in at the interval with a 12-2 lead, courtesy of tries from winger Wilf George – who seemed to have been tackled into touch – and hooker Seamus McCallion.

The huge St Helens support refused to write off their team, however, given their undoubted ability to score tries from anywhere on the field. Halifax would surely start to tire long before the final hooter. The second half was a real end-to-end affair laced with excitement and controversy. Mark Elia, in particular, proved to be a key figure in the destination of the trophy. His sizzling 75 yard try, a minute after the re-start, left full-back Eadie seemingly treading water in a desperate attempt to avert the inevitable. Loughlin's conversion reduced the arrears to 8-12. The rugged Australian made amends ten minutes later, however, with his side's third touchdown. At 8-18, things were slipping away from Murphy's Men. It was left to Paul Loughlin to keep the Saints in contention, with a marvellous individual try, using his winger, Barrie Ledger, as a foil. A drop-goal from Halifax loose-forward John Pendlebury gave his team a 12-19 advantage, only to be pegged back once more by Saints' substitute forward Paul Round, who crashed over and the Red and Whites were back in with more than a shout! By the 82nd minute it was only the drop-goal separating the sides, as Elia dived over the Halifax line once more. In a split-second, the quick-thinking Pendlebury managed to knock the ball from his grasp and the chance had gone. In Super League, a penalty try would ensue. Not in 1987! Three minutes later and another sweeping move saw the flying Kiwi touch down virtually in the same place only for referee Holdsworth to bring back play for a forward pass. As the seconds ticked away, the tactically naive Saints ignored the option of a drop-goal as a means of levelling the scores and went all out for the killer try which never came! Halifax were down and almost out as the final whistle sounded. The Saints would have surely finished the job in the replay at Old Trafford four days later – but it was not to be! Although an exasperated Alex Murphy pointed to some vital refereeing decisions which had gone against his team, this was one the Saints should have won in style!

Half time: 2-12
Receipts: £1,009,206 (The first 'million pound' final)

Lance Todd Trophy: G. Eadie (Halifax)

St Helens 18
Tries: Elia, Loughlin, Round
Goals: Loughlin (3)

Halifax 19
Tries: George, McCallion, Eadie
Goals: Whitfield (3)
Drop goal: Pendlebury

St Helens v. Halifax

Catastrophe! Halifax loose forward Pendlebury knocks the ball out of the grasp of Saints' centre mark Elia – and with it hopes of Challenge Cup Final success!

St Helens: P. Veivers; B. Ledger, P. Loughlin, M. Elia, K. McCormack; B. Clark, N. Holding; A. Burke, G. Liptrot, J. Fieldhouse, A. Platt, R. Haggerty, C. Arkwright (captain).
Subs: P. Round, P. Forber.

Halifax: G. Eadie; S. Wilson, C. Whitfield, G. Rix, W. George; C. Anderson (captain), G. Stephens; G. Beevers, S. Mc. Callion, K. Neller, P. Dixon, M. Scott, J. Pendlebury.
Subs: B. Juliff, N. James.

St Helens v. Wigan League Championship

27 December 1987
Central Park, Wigan

Attendance: 24,000
Referee: Mr Holdsworth (Kippax)

An act of escapology worthy of Harry Houdini or a Lazarus-like comeback from the dead might well sum up this remarkable victory by Saints over their arch-rivals in this Christmas cracker. For, remembering the 'no quarter asked or given' nature of these derby clashes, it beggared belief that a Saints team apparently sunk without trace in trailing 22-6 at half time should bounce back to grab the spoils, and leave Wigan point-less in the process. It was a tale of contrasting halves without doubt, with Rugby League scribes waxing lyrical of Saints coach Alex Murphy's interval pep talk, with its themes of self-belief along with a rallying call that if Wigan could score 22 points, so could Saints!

Murphy's men repaid his faith in them handsomely via a ruthlessly efficient display in the second 40 minutes, in which scrum-half Neil Holding quickly responded to his boss's instruction to run with the ball more. A famous victory from the jaws of defeat was taking place, with the howitzer boot of 'Lockers' regularly driving Wigan back, as well as being on target with six goals from seven attempts. Outstanding Australian full-back Phil Veivers also made a telling contribution, creating opportunities for a more expansive approach from the Saints. The kicking of centre Paul Loughlin (both tactical and with posts in sight) was also crucial as Saints snatched to their first win in five seasons at Central Park with two tries, (one a rare eight-pointer) plus a hand in two others, while Wigan and Coach Graeme Lowe were actually consigned to their heaviest defeat of the season.

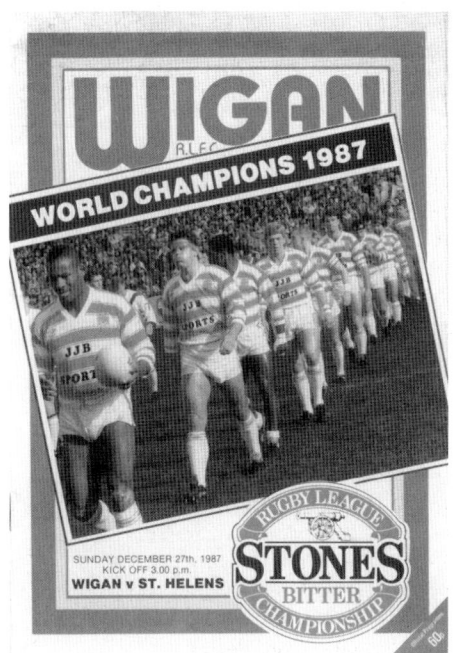

Now sadly no more, the time-honoured, if daunting stadium was a par-for-the-course seething cauldron when Wigan centre Joe Lydon opened the scoring with a penalty when Saints wandered off-side. But home joy was short-lived as the Veivers-Loughlin duo carved out a try for winger Kevin McCormack, with Loughlin's conversion giving the Saints a 6-2 lead with 15 minutes on the clock. Tragedy then struck for Saints when McCormack was stretchered off following a tackle by Adrian Shelford, and ex-Fylde star David Tanner came on as a replacement. It was at this point that shell-shocked Saints were put to the sword by the reigning champions, who scored four tries in 15 minutes through Kevin Iro, Andy Goodway, and two from Lydon, who also landed a further two goals. However, as the second half unfolded, it was readily apparent that Saints were in no mood for compromise despite their 16-point deficit, with what was arguably the turning point of a hitherto one-sided game coming with 50 minutes gone. It

Half time: 6-22

St Helens 32
Tries: Veivers (2), McCormack, Tanner, Quirk
Goals: Loughlin (6)

Wigan 22
Tries: Lydon (2), Iro, Goodway
Goal: Lydon (3)

ST HELENS v. WIGAN

Saints' Aussie full-back Phil Veivers was a fantastic servant to the Knowsley Road club and was at his brilliant best in the game against Wigan at Central Park with two sparkling tries. Safe as houses under the high ball and an excellent tactician, Veivers added much to Saints' attacking capabilities, making them one of the most attractive sides to watch in the late 1980s.

was then that a slick pass from Andy Platt sent Veivers over, and he was needlessly fouled in the act of touching down by Wigan captain Graeme West. The penalty was an 8-point try as Loughlin tacked on both goals from in front of the posts, and more's the pity that this deterrent to foul play has been expunged from the rule book.

A reborn Saints' side was now just 22-14 behind; they had the sniff of an unlikely victory and the fightback was on in earnest when Veivers crossed the Wigan line a second time after chasing a chip-through from his skipper Shane Cooper. Another towering conversion by Loughlin meant Saints were only two points adrift of wobbly Wigan and, with just 10 minutes remaining, a blindside break by Holding and supported by Veivers enabled substitute winger Tanner to inch Saints into a 24-22 advantage. Powerhouse Platt then set the seal on a truly terrific triumph over the Old Enemy by linking with Kiwi Mark Elia to send flying winger Les Quirk in for his fifteenth try of the season. Loughlin added a steepling goal from the touchline. With unexpected defeat looming, lack of discipline and frustration was evident in the Wigan ranks, and this manifested itself when the Cherry and Whites's skipper Ellery Hanley was sin-binned after a late tackle on the ubiquitous Holding. Loughlin rounded off a victory to savour for Saints and their loyal supporters with his sixth goal when Goodway was penalised for an offence on Paul Forber, while Wigan were left to eat humble pie by a Knowsley Road squad whose vocabulary simply did not include the word defeat.

St Helens: P. Veivers; K. McCormack, P. Loughlin, M. Elia, L. Quirk; S. Cooper (*captain*), N. Holding; A. Burke, P. Groves, P. Souto, P. Forber, R. Haggerty, A. Platt.
Subs: D. Tanner, S. Evans.

Wigan: S. Hampson; D. Marshall, J. Lydon, E. Hanley, K. Iro; S. Edwards, A. Gregory; I. Lucas, M. Dermott, B. Case, G. West (*captain*), I. Potter, A. Goodway.
Subs: R. Russell, A. Shelford.

St Helens v. Leeds John Player Trophy final

9 January 1988
Central Park, Wigan

Attendance: 16,669
Referee: Mr Lindop (Wakefield)

The 1987/88 campaign saw the St Helens board – and coach Alex Murphy – search far and wide for talent in order to build a team capable of challenging for top honours. Stuart Evans, a former Welsh Rugby Union international prop, joined from Neath; hooker Paul 'Kit Kat' Groves from Salford and flying winger Les Quirk from Barrow, for a £55,000 fee. The most vital signing, however, was Kiwi stand-off Shane Cooper, who arrived at Knowsley Road after touring with Auckland, in mid-November. The arrival of the twenty-seven-year-old master tactician coincided with the team's best rugby of the campaign, climaxed by a memorable victory in the John Player Trophy final – the only major honour that had eluded the St Helens club in its long history. This was a more disciplined Saints from the 'devil-may-care' approach of the previous months. A tremendous defensive display in the second half of a breath-taking contest saw them through, as the Loiners fought desperately to get back on terms, without success.

The two evenly-matched sides produced two tries and three goals, the difference proving to be a 38th minute drop-goal from scrum-half Neil Holding, who had a storming game in the Central Park mud. Yet it was centre Paul Loughlin who was a clear choice as man of the match, with two superb tries. His display that afternoon did much to secure his selection for the 1988 tour to Australia, together with team-mates Paul Groves, Roy Haggerty and Andy Platt.

It was big-spending Leeds, with four Australians in their ranks, who scored first, courtesy of a converted try from stand-off David Creasser. Paul Loughlin booted over a penalty, followed by a surging run ending between the posts to give Saints the lead – despite strong appeals for a double-movement! A Creasser penalty goal kept the Loiners in with a shout and Leeds capitalised after second-rower Peter Souto lost the ball in his own half. Maskill fed Creasser, who set up Australian superstar Peter Jackson for a classy four-pointer. The conversion gave Leeds a 14-8 advantage, reduced by Holding's crucial 'drop' just before half time.

It was the Saints who grasped the nettle after just two minutes of the restart! A flowing move out wide involving Platt and Forber saw rangy centre Paul Loughlin cut inside in classic fashion, leaving Basnett and Australian full-back Marty Gurr trailing in his wake en route to the Leeds posts. He belted over the conversion for good measure, putting St Helens 15-14 ahead. The Leeds forwards continually drove into the Saints' half as the game went on, but to no avail. Their only real threats came from two attempted drop-goals, by Ashton and Schofield, both of which failed to break the deadlock, although Schofield's effort did hit an upright seven minutes before the final hooter. Normally renowned for their attacking prowess, it was defensive steel which proved to be the match-winner, with second-rower Andy Platt making an incredible 43 tackles! It was to be coach Alex Murphy's finest hour in his spell at Knowsley Road, after a truly epic encounter, in front of a huge national television audience – the perfect advert for the 'Greatest Game'!

Half time: 9-14   John Player Special Man of the Match: Paul Loughlin (St Helens)

St Helens 15
Tries: Loughlin (2)
Goals: Loughlin (3)
Drop goals: Holding

Leeds 14
Tries: Jackson, Creasser
Goals: Creasser (3)

St Helens v. Leeds

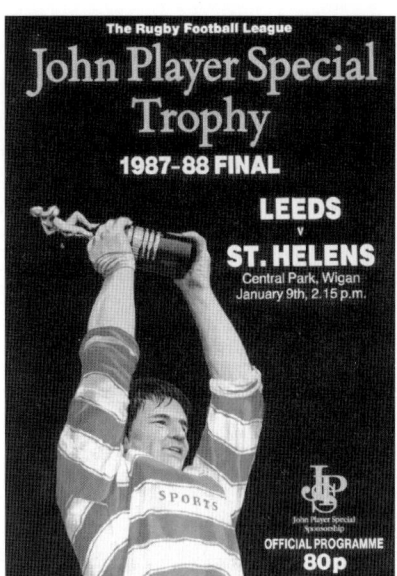

Next stop Australia! Saints' centre Paul Loughlin powers his way to the line, leaving Leeds' Australian full-back Marty Gurr on the Central Park turf. Dave Tanner (left) and Paul Forber are the two other Saints in the picture.

St Helens: P. Vievers; D. Tanner, P. Loughlin, M. Elia, L. Quirk; S. Cooper (*captain*), N. Holding; T. Burke, P. Groves, P. Souto, P. Forber, R. Haggerty, A. Platt.
Subs: D. Large, S. Evans.

Leeds: M. Gurr; S. Morris, G. Schofield, P. Jackson, D. Basnett; D. Creasser, R. Ashton; P. Tunks (*captain*), C. Maskill, K. Rayne, R. Powell, P. Medley, D. Heron.
Subs: C. Gibson, K. Fairbank.

ST HELENS v. WARRINGTON Challenge Cup Second Round

13 February 1988
Wilderspool Stadium, Warrington

Attendance: 9,500
Referee: Mr Holdsworth (Kippax)

A real blood and thunder clash on a glue-pot pitch at Wilderspool thrilled an enthusiastic crowd and a huge television audience – everything that you would want from a Challenge Cup tie and more! The Saints, under coach Alex Murphy, were determined to reach the Challenge Cup final to give their supporters some success after their demise against Halifax at Wembley twelve months before. Yet they were made to fight all the way by a dogged Warrington outfit who were within two minutes of pulling off a well-earned victory. The Wires opened the scoring in the first few minutes, with full-back Brian Johnson interchanging passes with winger Dave Lyon, who raced over in the corner. Woods' conversion scraped over past the post. The Saints fought back quickly with a brilliant try from Paul Forber, who got on the end of a superb Loughlin break in the centre of the field and dived over in flamboyant fashion. In a fast, open cup-tie, the tries kept on coming as the scores changed hands several times. Warrington loose forward Billy McGinty strolled through a gaping hole in the Saints' defence for Woods to convert with an excellent kick from the touchline for a 10-6 lead. The Warrington pack, with Boyd, Jackson and Gregory prominent, did the necessary spadework and scrum-half Holden put in a tantalising chip from the 20-metre line, which Woods followed up and beat Veivers to the touchdown, for the third try in what was still the first quarter. It was Saints' turn to reply with another stunning sequence of attacking football. From a tap penalty on the right, the ball went down the line to the effervescent Roy Haggerty, who made a half-break, and fed Veivers. Following great combination from centres Loughlin and Elia, the move was finished off by Les Quirk close to the corner flag. The score remained at 14-10 to Warrington at the interval. Meanwhile, both sets of supporters changed ends – a veritable tidal wave of humanity, giving the stewards a giant headache – something that is now outlawed at Wilderspool! Warrington, who lost their inspirational captain Les Boyd during the first half with a broken arm, faced an intensive Saints bombardment. The pressure told, as hard-running second-rower Roy Haggerty punched a hole twenty metres out and fed the supporting Fieldhouse, who crashed over unopposed. Loughlin's simple conversion gave the Saints a two-point advantage. Yet there was to be another twist in this see-saw encounter, when Des Drummond, with his typical 'head down' running style, smashed his way past Phil Veivers for a vital four-pointer. As Veivers received the 'magic sponge' Woods's 'flapper' conversion did just enough to go over the bar – 20-16 to the Wire! Dave Tanner booted over a crucial penalty shortly after to reduce the margin and it was time for a real 'Grandstand finish'! Two minutes to go and Paul Groves worked a run-around move with Neil Holding. He gave an outrageous dummy and raced into space near the Warrington line. As he was tackled just short, he put out a terrific pass to the supporting John Fieldhouse, who plunged over! Loughlin converted, to give the Saints a fantastic victory in a truly classic match. Yet the march to Wembley was halted unceremoniously for Murphy's Army at the Willows in the next round, as Salford produced a sensational 22-18 success. The unpredictability of the Challenge Cup was always one of its greatest strengths!

Half time: 10-14

St Helens 24
Tries: Fieldhouse (2), Quirk, Forber
Goals: Tanner (3), Loughlin

Warrington 20
Tries: Lyon, McGinty, Woods, Drummond
Goals: Woods (2)

ST HELENS v. WARRINGTON

One of the key moments in the Warrington-Saints cup-tie. Wires' Australian captain Les Boyd is attended to by the Trainer and had to leave the field with a recurrence of a broken arm. Fellow prop Bob Jackson takes a breather on his haunches, while the Saints forwards get ready to pack down, from left to right: Stuart Evans, Paul Groves, Tony Burke, John Fieldhouse and Paul Forber. Referee John Holdsworth waits to restart play.

St Helens: P. Veivers; D. Tanner, P. Loughlin, M. Elia, L. Quirk; S. Cooper (*captain*), N. Holding; A. Burke, P. Groves, S. Evans, P. Forber, R. Haggerty, C. Arkwright.
Subs: B. Dwyer, J. Fieldhouse.

Warrington: B. Johnson; D. Drummond, P. Cullen, J. Ropati, D. Lyon; J. Woods, K. Holden; L. Boyd (*captain*), C. Webb, B. Jackson, M. Roberts, M. Gregory, B. McGinty.
Subs: R. Duane, G. Sanderson.

St Helens v. Widnes Challenge Cup semi-final

11 March 1989
Central Park, Wigan

Attendance: 17,119
Referee: Mr Holdsworth (Kippax)

It is quite unusual for the Saints to be classed as underdogs, but that's what they were for this semi-final clash at Wigan. Mighty Widnes were at their peak, defending First Division champions, with a three-quarter line packed with pace and a mobile pack. Yet no side coached by Alex Murphy could ever be discounted, as the crowd of over 17,000 found out. It was a superb match, with both sides willing to play attractive, open football. Although St Helens had been hit by injuries, Widnes were without their Welsh stand-off star Jonathan Davies, with powerful prop Kurt Sorensen on the bench. At full-back for the Saints was seventeen-year-old Gary Connolly, who had kept his amateur status so that he could tour Down Under with the BARLA youth squad at the end of the season! He was not out of his depth by any means! It was the Saints who made the most of the early exchanges, enjoying territory and possession in abundance. After nine minutes, they took the lead when Cumbrian left-winger Les Quirk forced his way over in the corner, despite the efforts of Currier and Thackray to halt his progress. This was Quirk's 100th career try and the tenth successive match in which he had scored – a Saints' club record! Although Loughlin missed the conversion, St Helens were seemingly in control, with half-backs Holding and Bloor controlling the midfield. Yet Widnes surged forward with a break from Grima on half-way, who gave centre Wright a difficult pass to handle before the centre stormed in between the posts after 13 minutes, converted by Currier to level matters at 6-6. Then came a huge slice of luck! Holding scooted from acting half back just over halfway and wrong-footed Richie Eyres to such an extent that the Widnes player tripped his opponent. Referee Holdsworth had no hesitation but to point to the dressing room! This was a huge psychological, as well as numerical advantage for Murphy's men. The Saints were playing out of their skins at this stage and Quirk was denied a second try in the corner by the touch judge's flag.

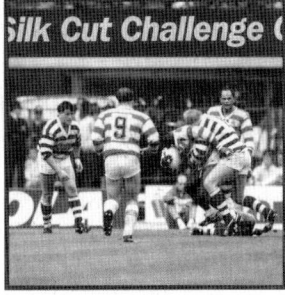

1988/89 SEMI-FINAL
ST. HELENS v WIDNES
CENTRAL PARK, WIGAN
MARCH 11th 1989 3.00pm
PRICE 80p

Widnes banged over a penalty just before the break after a high tackle by Bloor on David Hulme, but there was more to come! Shane Cooper instigated a break on the left, carried on by Connolly who kicked ahead. Widnes full-back Alan Tait had no option but to kick it dead and from the resulting drop out, prop Paul Forber off-loaded brilliantly for scrum-half Bloor to race over from 15 yards to the line. Loughlin's conversion gave the Saints a 12-8 advantage at half time.

The action continued unabated after the restart and it was Widnes who took the lead in the 47th minute, with giant Tongan forward Koloto dummying and holding the ball up for David Hulme to go over by the posts – a move quite similar to the St Helens score before the interval. Saints tried desperately to get back in the match and Quirk was unlucky

Half time: 12-8

St Helens 16
Tries: Quirk (2), Bloor
Goals: Loughlin (2)

Widnes 14
Tries: D. Hulme, Wright
Goals: Currier (3)

St Helens v. Widnes

The key moment of the 1989 Challenge Cup semi-final! Centre Paul Loughlin breaks through the Widnes defence before feeding winger Les Quirk, who barged his way over in the corner. Andy Currier is the Widnes player in desperate pursuit.

to have the ball knocked out by Thackray as the line beckoned. In the last few minutes, however, hooker Groves picked up at acting half back and made one of his trademark breaks before feeding the long-striding Paul Loughlin just inside the 25. The Great Britain centre's pass to Quirk was timed to perfection, just giving him enough room to power his way over in the corner, despite the attention of two desperate cover defenders. St Helens were in front! Loughlin's conversion sailed to the left of the posts, but it did not matter. The Saints had pulled off a magnificent victory, seemingly against all the odds in a truly pulsating encounter, with the lead changing hands five times! On the final whistle, hundreds of delighted Saints fans invaded the pitch. Paul Groves was carried shoulder high through the throng at one point. Coach Alex Murphy managed to get his words out to an exasperated BBC reporter, despite much jubilation and back-slapping. 'I'm absolutely delighted,' he exclaimed. 'That's what no hopers get. You keep trying and you never know!' Amen to that. Although Wigan put an end to hopes of Challenge Cup success at Wembley, this backs to the wall performance – and Les Quirk's sensational late try – will never be forgotten by those who witnessed it.

St Helens: G. Connolly; D. Tanner, P. Veivers, P. Loughlin, L. Quirk; N. Holding, D. Bloor; A. Burke, P. Groves, P. Forber, D. Harrison, R. Haggerty, S. Cooper (*captain*).
Subs: M. Bailey, P. Jones.

Widnes: A. Tait; R. Thackray, A. Currier, D. Wright, M. Offiah; D. Hulme (*captain*), P. Hulme; J. Grima, P. McKenzie, D. Pyke, M. O'Neill, E. Koloto, R. Eyres.
Subs: B. Dowd, K. Sorenson.

ST HELENS v. NEW ZEALAND Tour Match

1 October 1989　　　　　　　　　　Attendance: 6,940
Knowsley Road, St Helens　　　　　Referee: Mr R. Tennant (Castleford)

Barnstorming forward Paul Forber scored 50 tries in a 10-year career with Saints, but none more crucial than the one in this epic clash against the visiting Kiwis. For, with just three minutes to play and Saints trailing 26-23, the Thatto Heath lad dubbed 'Buffer' by supporters snatched victory from the jaws of defeat when he plunged across the New Zealand line. The Knowsley Road faithful erupted at this apparent late winner, but the drama had not ended, as Kiwi stand-off Kelly Shelford was off-target with a last-gasp penalty kick which would have swung the pendulum back New Zealand's way.

Having suffered three defeats in four games early in the 1989 season, an injury-hit Saints' side fielding debutant Andy Bateman were seen as sacrificial lambs to the slaughter in tackling a touring team that was almost at full strength. 'Comeback Kings' Saints thought differently, however, and this up-lifting display of guts, determination and will-to-win had Coach Alex Murphy waxing lyrical at the final whistle on the opening fixture of the Kiwi tour.

Fixture-wise, it all began as long ago as 1907, when the trail-blazing Kiwis defeated Saints 24-5 at Knowsley Road, and there have been several stirring encounters since, including a 15-7 win by the tourists in 1939 before the Second World War intervened. Eight long years elapsed before New Zealand graced Knowsley Road once more in 1947 and emerged victorious yet again, this time to the tune of 11-5. Albert 'Sonny' Doyle scored a 50-yard try for Saints. The most humiliating defeat for Saints by New Zealand came via a 46-8 thrashing in 1985, so it will be understood that a revenge motive was in mind four years later when, ironically, Saints were skippered by Kiwi Shane Cooper. Antipodean links do not end there, for the time-honoured trio of New Zealanders Lou Hutt, Trevor Hall and Roy Hardgrave played for Saints in the 1930s; Saints ventured to Auckland in 1985 and former Kiwi full-back Mike McClennan held the coaching reins at Knowsley Road between 1990 and 1993. A cursory glance at the 1989 squad reveals that several found the attractions of the domestic game irresistible in joining English clubs. These include Mark Elia, Tea Ropati and Kevin Iro, all of whom played for Saints.

Back to that crisp October afternoon in 1989, however. Saints raced into a 6-0 lead with an interception try from Alan Hunte and converted by David Tanner, before Neil Holding dropped a goal that ultimately proved decisive. New Zealand grabbed an 8-7 lead with a try and two goals from Kelly Shelford and when Elia jetted 60 yards to touch down, Shelford's subsequent conversion meant the visitors led 14-7 at half time. Saints reduced the arrears with a second goal from Tanner on the restart, and the scene was then set for Cooper's men to regain the initiative in rousing fashion. This came courtesy of Welsh prop and man of the match Stuart Evans, whose unstoppable burst over the New Zealand line saw Tanner add the extra points. The shell-shocked Kiwis hit back with further tries by Iro and Elia, and with Shelford converting both, New Zealand were back in front by 26-17 as the match entered its final quarter. However, there was light at the end of the tunnel for Saints when Mark Bailey and Phil Veivers combined to send Tanner over, and the ex-Fylde star cut Saints' arrears to three points and boosted his points tally to 14 with the goal kick. 'Cometh the hour, cometh the man,' as in stepped Forber…and the rest, as they say, is history!

Half time: 7-14

St Helens 27
Tries: Hunte, Evans, Tanner, Forber
Goals: Tanner (5)
Drop goal: Holding

New Zealand 26
Tries: Elia (2), Iro, K. Shelford
Goals: K. Shelford (5)

St Helens v. New Zealand

Centre Kevin Iro dives over the line for his second half touchdown, despite the attentions of Saints' Alan Hunte, but ultimately in vain, as New Zealand were pipped at the post with Paul Forber's late try. The big Kiwi centre signed for St Helens towards the end of his career and did much to bring further success to the club in the Super League competition at the turn of the 20th century.

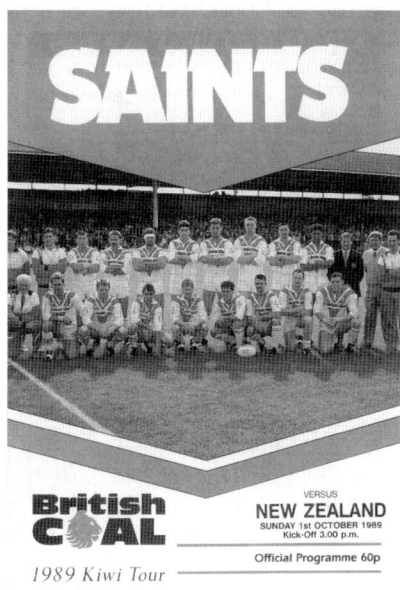

St Helens: P. Veivers; D. Large, R. Haggerty, A. Hunte, D. Tanner; M. Bailey, N. Holding; S. Evans, P. Groves, A. Bateman, P. Forber, D. Cosgrove, S. Cooper (*captain*).
Subs: P. Jones, A. Donegan.

New Zealand: D. Williams; G. Mercer, D. Watson, K. Iro, M. Elia; K. Shelford, G. Freeman; A. Shelford, D. Mann, J. Goulding, S. Stewart, E. Faimalo, H. McGahan (*captain*).
Subs: P. Bancroft, T. Nikau.

St Helens v. Widnes Challenge Cup semi-final

30 March 1991
Central Park, Wigan

Attendance: 16,109
Referee: Mr Holdsworth (Kippax)

Widnes were the Team of All the Talents in 1991, with an uncompromising forward pack and a devastating three-quarter line, including the likes of Martin Offiah, capable of scoring tries from anywhere on the field. St Helens were capable of playing marvellous football on their day, yet were classed as underdogs for this Challenge Cup semi-final. After all, Widnes were eager to avenge their shock defeat at the hands of the Saints at the same stage two years before. Full-back Alan Tait and stand-off Tony Myler were crucial absentees for the men from Naughton Park, while Saints coach Mike McClennan started with Bernard Dwyer at hooker in place of Paul Groves, who was on the bench. Even from the first series of bone-crushing tackles, it was obvious that St Helens were no push-overs, moving up quickly to try and keep the ball away from the Widnes three-quarter line. It was Widnes' Jon Davies, a shock selection in the centre, who had the chance of the first points. Yet two penalty attempts both hit the woodwork and went wide. This was a riveting contest, where the Saints forwards, particularly props Ward and George Mann, smashed into the Widnes defensive line from deep and caused all manner of problems. It was St Helens who took the lead, courtesy of a Paul Loughlin penalty after referee Holdsworth had penalised Widnes scrum-half Paul Hulme for the use of an elbow. Loughlin's goal gave the Saints a two-point cushion which they held until just before the interval, when Davies's third penalty attempt hit the woodwork again, but this time went over – much to the relief of the Widnes outfit, who had been totally out-played by their opponents.

The Saints pack continued to dominate after the interval, although chances for both sides were hardly of the clear cut variety. Scrum-half Paul Bishop was a veritable terrier in loose play, with fellow half-back Jonathan Griffiths enjoying his best game for the club. Fittingly, it was the former Llanelli man's try which swung the game Saints' way just after the restart courtesy of some brilliant running from Alan Hunte, Harrison and Ward. Paul Bishop's kick through was expertly read by George Mann on the Widnes 20-metre line, who picked up and fed Griffiths steaming through on the inside – a try which set the Saints on the road to Wembley! Loughlin's conversion gave his team an 8-2 lead, although it took a magnificent take from Veivers to defuse a towering bomb from Jon Davies under his own crossbar.

Yet it was Saints who scored again midway through the second half – a magnificent take by Alan Hunte from Bishop's towering last tackle bomb, which really demoralised the Chemics. At 14-2, the Saints really started to throw the ball about. John Harrison was stopped inches from the line after a brilliant 20 metre burst. Widnes switched Jon Davies to stand-off, but it was too late! Then

Half time: 2-2

St Helens 19
Tries: Griffiths (2), Hunte
Goals: Loughlin (3)
Drop goal: Groves

Widnes 2
Goal: Davies

St Helens v. Widnes

Saints Welsh half-back Jon Griffiths played a massive part in his team's demolition of much fancied Widnes in an epic second-half display at Central Park.

came the best try of this pulsating encounter. Mann began the move in his own half; Groves went from dummy half with a one-handed off-load to Cooper. He carried on the move to Veivers going right, on to the rampaging Kevin Ward and a slipped pass to Ropati on the 20-metre line. The New Zealand centre produced a fabulous off-load to Griffiths in support on the outside, before the Welsh Wizard completed the touchdown with a joyful dive over the line. What a try – a reflection of his team's total control of the proceedings! Although Paul Loughlin failed with the conversion, a Paul Groves drop-goal sealed a worthy place in the Challenge Cup final for Mike McClennan's men. Man of the Match Jon Griffiths was carried shoulder high to the dressing rooms by delirious Saints' fans after his superb two-try performance. Yet it had been a brilliant team effort and one which will never be forgotten by anyone who was present on that overcast day at Central Park in 1991.

St Helens: P. Veivers, A. Hunte, T. Ropati, P. Loughlin, L. Quirk; J. Griffiths, P. Bishop; J. Neill, B. Dwyer, K. Ward, J. Harrison, G. Mann, S. Cooper (*captain*).
Subs: M. Bailey, P. Groves.

Widnes: S. Spruce, J. Devereux, A. Currier, J. Davies, M. Offiah; D. Hulme (*captain*), P. Hulme; K. Sorenson, P. McKenzie, E. Faimalo, R. Eyres, E. Koloto, L. Holliday.
Subs: J. Grima, S. McCurrie.

St Helens v. Wigan Lancashire Cup semi-final

10 October 1991
Knowsley Road, St Helens

Attendance: 17,125
Referee: Mr R. Whitfield (Widnes)

Painful memories of two Wembley defeats must have been erased from Saintly memory banks after this magnificent Lancashire Cup semi-final conquest of the World Champions. A first-half defensive effort of Rorke's Drift dimensions, bolstered by the first three of five tries from the top drawer, provided Saints with a rock-like foundation for success. On a night when all were heroes, indestructible prop Kevin Ward, nursing all manner of injuries, rose from the treatment table to earn the man of the match award, which typified the team spirit that prevailed at Knowsley Road in 1991. Another bonus came with the commanding performance of Gary Connolly, who gave tour selectors his broadest hint yet with centre three-quarter play of a very high order indeed. But arguably the key to the ultimate triumph lay with scrum-half Paul Bishop who – revelling in the captaincy role in the absence of Shane Cooper – succeeded admirably in his bid to close down opposite number and fellow skipper Andy Gregory.

The cauldron-like atmosphere of these derby clashes was evident from kick-off, with Bishop quickly falling foul of referee Whitfield after a play-the-ball incident with Frano Botica, who was off-target with the ensuing penalty kick. Saints, however, showed immediate inclination to give the ball air, and gained an early foothold with a try from barnstorming Paul Forber, who plunged over after brilliant handling involving Ward, Bishop, Tea Ropati and George Mann. Smarting from this reverse, Wigan camped on the Saints line for ten nerve-wracking minutes but the uncompromising home side held the Riversiders at bay as Botica limped off to be replaced by Mike Forshaw. Gus O'Donnell for McGinty became a further substitution in the visitor's ranks, as Saints proceeded to stomp their authority on the game with a brace of tries which were sheer class, both in build-up and execution. Stand-off Phil Veivers triggered the first before releasing right-wing pair Connolly and Mike Riley, who inter-passed in a fashion reminiscent of 1961 Wembley stalwarts Ken Large and Tom Van Vollenhoven, before Connolly, like Vol, raced over the Wigan line. Full-back David Tanner, a revelation since being restored to the side, tacked on the conversion and the former Fylde Rugby Union player then surged through to send winger Anthony Sullivan over in the corner after a heart-stopping juggling act with the ball. Wigan brought back McGinty for stand-off Edwards on the restart, only to see Saints consolidate further with a try created by Tanner, Mann and Connolly and finished by Riley, who swept inside full-back Hampson with the assurance of a racing thoroughbred. Gregory had a brief moment of freedom in laying on a defence-splitting pass for centre Sam Panapa to score, but prospects of a Wigan fight-back faded when Saints loose forward Bernard Dwyer nipped over from a scrum for Tanner to convert. Replacement of Connolly by Mark Bailey heralded snap drop-goals by Bishop and Forber, the first a steepling 35-yarder, the other dispatched when Forber was travelling at a rare old rate of knots. Tanner added a penalty after Paul Groves had been held down in the tackle, before Ward left the arena to a reception reserved for gladiators as substitute David Lever joined the fray. Wigan staged their late, late show with touchdowns from O'Donnell and McGinty, plus a conversion by Lydon, leaving the bumper crowd to reflect on what had been an absorbing encounter, whatever their allegiance.

Half time: 16-6

St Helens 28
Tries: Forber, Connolly, Sullivan, Riley, Dwyer
Goals: Tanner (3)
Drop goals: Bishop, Forber

Wigan 16
Tries: Panapa, O'Donnell, McGinty
Goals: Lydon (2)

St Helens v. Wigan

Simply unstoppable! Saints' Kiwi forward George Mann takes the game to Wigan. Notice his distinctive running style.

St Helens: D. Tanner; M. Riley, G. Connolly, T. Ropati, A. Sullivan; P. Veivers, P. Bishop (*captain*); J. Neill, P. Groves, K. Ward, P. Forber, G. Mann, B. Dwyer.
Subs: M. Bailey, D. Lever.

Wigan: S. Hampson; D. Myers, S. Panapa, J. Lydon, F. Botica; S. Edwards, A. Gregory (*captain*); N. Cowie, W. McGinty, A. Platt, D. Betts, I. Gildart, G. Miles.
Subs: A. O'Donnell, M. Forshaw.

St Helens v. Leeds Challenge Cup Second Round

8 February 1992
Headingley, Leeds

Attendance: 9,610
Referee: Mr Whitfield (Widnes)

This was one to savour. It provided a national audience on Grandstand with a veritable demonstration of all that is so admired about the Saints' style of rugby at its best – great support play, the ball spread to the wings at every opportunity and some devastating handling skills. Yet it was Leeds' young captain, Bobbie Goulding, who got proceedings under way with a towering 35-metre drop-goal! The Saints then responded with one of the greatest tries in their history! Sonny Nickle drove the ball out from his own 25 and fed Griffiths; on to Dwyer, then wide to Gary Connolly on the South Stand touchline. He brought Hunte into action just before halfway, who passed out of the tackle inside to Dwyer; on to Griffiths; a diving pass to Bishop, who found Cooper in support. The wily Skipper fed Anthony Sullivan at pace in the left centre position, who drew a defender and passed to Ropati, who checked back inside. A magnificent flipped pass to Shane Cooper and this marvellous sequence of support play ended with a fantastic four-pointer, converted by Paul Bishop.

Big-spending Leeds, without key stars Schofield and Ellery Hanley, got back into the match after Carl Gibson charged down Veivers' clearance kick in the centre of the field and dived over at the Scoreboard End. Saints soon managed to regain the lead with a try from twenty-year-old centre Gary Connolly, who forced his way over despite the efforts of three Leeds defenders. Goulding squared matters at 8-8 with another virtually identical drop-goal, yet when second-rower O'Neill knocked on in his own twenty-five, it was to prove costly for the Yorkshiremen. It was Shane Cooper who picked up from the scrum and using Bishop and Nickle as a foil, shrugged off his opposite number Divorty and strolled over for a superb try, to give his side a four point lead at half time.

SILK CUT CHALLENGE CUP

SECOND ROUND
LEEDS v. ST HELENS
Saturday, 8th February, 1992
Kick-off: 2.15 p.m.
Official Programme: £1

Saints' tactics of exposing Leeds' frail defence out wide was certainly paying off, with Hunte roaring into space on the left and firing the ball out wide to Anthony Sullivan, as he was tackled by Ford. Sully positively roared in from 30 metres, rounding full-back Morvin Edwards en route to the line. Bishop's conversion made it 18-8 to the visitors after 51 minutes of superb rugby league football. Leeds' prop Molloy ran in an amazing 30-yard try, just when every Saints defender thought he was going to pass and it was time for the visitors to step up a gear once more. Groves, Bishop and Ward, with a brilliant lofted pass, combined to put Connolly in for a try in the corner. Bishop's conversion gave the Saints a 12-point cushion and there was no stopping them now! Eleven minutes to go and Kevin Ward picked up at acting half-back and punched a huge hole in the defence on half way. A pass to the supporting Cooper, on to

Half time: 12-8

St Helens 32
Tries: Cooper (2), Connolly (2), Sullivan (2), Hunte
Goals: Bishop (2)

Leeds 12
Tries: Gibson, Molloy
Goal: Goulding
Drop goals: Goulding (2)

St Helens v. Leeds

Skipper Shane Cooper initiates another attack at Headingley. The New Zealand playmaker was one of the main influences in Saints' stunning 32-12 success, contributing two tries in the process! Scrum-half Paul Bishop runs in support, a tough, aggressive and durable number seven. Towering second-rower John Harrison is in the background, a member of a highly mobile forward pack on the day.

Hunte and the inevitable four points!

The Saints were in rampant form now and in the last few minutes came another bewildering exhibition of support play. Scrum-half Bishop broke up to half-way...a pass to Ropati...on to hooker Groves steaming up in support and a final lobbed pass to Sullivan who ran in from 15 metres. 'Sheer pace and support play at its best,' exclaimed commentator Ray French. Bishop once again was wide with the conversion, perhaps the only slight disappointment on the day, with two successful kicks from seven attempts. But what a match – and with only three penalties during the 80 minutes for good measure. The 32-12 margin was the most points Leeds had conceded at Headingley in a Challenge Cup tie in their history. Yet even their staunchest supporters had to agree that there was so much to admire in Saints' 32-12 success – the power of Kevin Ward, the guile of skipper Shane Cooper, hard-working half-backs and the sheer pace of wingers Hunte and Sullivan out wide, scintillating support play and more besides. Yet it was to be a disappointing exit at Knowsley Road in the Third Round against Wigan, when the home side dropped far too much ball. Wigan were seasoned cup campaigners and, whether we wanted to accept it or not, had the winning habit when it really mattered.

St Helens: P. Veivers; A. Hunte, G. Connolly, T. Ropati, A. Sullivan; J. Griffiths, P. Bishop; J. Harrison, P. Groves, K. Ward, S. Nickle, B. Dwyer, S. Cooper (captain).
Subs: M. Riley, P. Forber.

Leeds: M. Edwards; P. Ford, D. Creaser, C. Gibson, J. Bentley, C. Innes; B. Goulding (captain), C. Heugh, C. Maskill, S. Wane, M. O'Neill, P. Dixon, G. Divorty.
Subs: G. Stephens, S. Molloy.

St Helens v. Leeds

Above: All so easy! Saints' centre Gary Connolly strolls over for the first of his two tries at Headingley. A superb all-round centre three-quarter, who could also operate at full-back, it was a severe blow to Saints' team-building plans when he signed for deadly rivals Wigan for the start of the 1993/94 campaign.

Opposite: What a photograph! It encapsulates the strength and power of one of the world's greatest prop forwards – the mighty Kevin Ward. The former Castleford stalwart enjoyed a tremendous Indian summer at Knowsley Road and became a hugely popular figure with the fans. Ward was in tremendous form during the Headingley cup-tie and is seen battling his way past two would-be tacklers in the lead-up to Alan Hunte's try late in the match. Kevin's career was to finish tragically with a leg injury at Central Park in a league match some twelve months later – yet he will never be forgotten for his deeds on the club and international front.

St Helens v. Leeds

St Helens v. Wigan Stones Bitter Championship

27 December 1992
Knowsley Road, St Helens

Attendance: 17,495
Referee: Mr Whitfield (Widnes)

Spellbinding Saints gave their faithful fans the Christmas bonus they had yearned with a performance that almost exceeded superlatives. When the visitors raced into a six-point lead in the fourth minute, shocked Saints supporters wondered if the floodgates would open – and so they did! What happened next is etched indelibly in Knowsley Road folklore as Wigan were taken apart in a seven-try demolition act of high-speed riveting rugby league. The epic victory – Saints' biggest against Wigan at Knowsley Road since the Second World War– was also sweet music for a side relishing a first League win over the Old Enemy since Good Friday 1990, and who had not enjoyed the rub of the green versus Wigan in recent seasons. The defeat was the first Wigan had suffered away from home since losing at Salford in November 1991, and also signalled the end of a nine-match Championship-winning run that season, while Queensland were the only side to notch 40 points against Wigan in the previous decade! Saints and their fans were on Cloud Nine after coming within striking distance of scoring 50 points against Wigan, and they might well have reached the half-century for the first time since 1969 but for wayward goal-kicking which saw a dozen points go begging.

The Riversiders set the scoreboard in motion when Andy Platt broke John Harrison's tackle and Shaun Edwards, Martin Crompton and Martin Offiah supported to send Frano Botica over in the Scoreboard Corner, with the ex-All Black adding a superb conversion. Knowsley Road was no place for the faint-hearted as resilient Saints set about retrieving the situation with George Mann, Sonny Nickle and Chris Joynt posing problems with tremendous bursts in a team perpetually going forward.

It was former Oldham forward Joynt who established the bridgehead for Saints' opening try with a barnstorming break before being halted by Botica, but Cooper's shrewd pass sent Alan Hunte in by the corner flag. The departure of Offiah with a shoulder injury saw Wigan introduce Jason Robinson, and moments later Saints grabbed the initiative when Mann, Cooper and Hunte set up position for Nickle to dive over with Loughlin converting. Cracks were now appearing in a Wigan defence striving to cope with Saints' squad playing like men possessed. They moved into a 16-6 lead when Cooper, Mann, Gary Connolly and Dave Lyon sent Hunte in for his second try, with Loughlin goaling.

Kiwis Jarrod McCracken and Tea Ropati also proved thorns in Wigan's side and it was Ropati's blistering break and an adroit Bernard Dwyer pass, which sent Joynt under the posts for Loughlin to add the extra points. 'Lockers' then set the seal on a first half for

Half time: 24-6

St Helens 41
Tries: Hunte (2), Nickle (2), Joynt, Lyon, Ropati
Goals: Loughlin (6)
Drop goal: O'Donnell

Wigan 6
Try: Botica
Goal: Botica

St Helens v. Wigan

Saints' Great Britain second-rower Sonny Nickle, who scored two crucial tries in the crushing defeat of Wigan in 1992.

ecstasy for Saints' supporters with a penalty goal after Kelvin Skerrett was cautioned, with the air of buoyancy at a 24-6 interval lead extending to the PA system plea to Saints' fans not to encroach onto the pitch to congratulate their team at the final whistle!

The announcer's confidence was not misplaced as Lyon increased Saints' advantage with a try on the restart, and there was by now more of a hint of desperation in the Wigan approach to an ominous situation. This manifested itself when Skerrett was sent off following a high tackle on McCracken, and a further breach of the peace involving Nickle and Platt saw referee Whitfield brandish the yellow card. Loughlin's boot pushed Saints into a 30-6 lead when Crompton fouled Mann, who then found himself sin-binned for an offence on Phil Clarke. Phil Veivers joined the Saints' ranks as substitute for Ropati at this point. There was no slackening of effort by Saints as they strove – albeit unsuccessfully – for sufficient victory margin to ensure pole position in the table as the game entered a final quarter highlighted by further touchdowns by Nickle and Ropati. A drop-goal from substitute Gus 'Ducky' O'Donnell and Loughlin's last goal rounded off the scoring after an afternoon of unashamed euphoria for the Knowsley Road faithful, when even the absence of suspended legend Kevin Ward was scarcely felt such was the commitment of the fantastic fifteen that took the field.

St Helens: D. Lyon; J. McCracken, G. Connolly, P. Loughlin, A. Hunte; T. Ropati, S. Cooper (*captain*); J. Neill, B. Dwyer, J. Harrison, G. Mann, S. Nickle, C. Joynt.
Subs: A. O'Donnell, P. Veivers.

Wigan: S. Hampson; S. Panapa, D. Bell (*captain*), A. Farrar, M. Offiah; S. Edwards, F. Botica; N. Cowie, M. Crompton, K. Skerrett, D. Betts, A. Platt, P. Clarke.
Subs: J. Robinson, W. McGinty.

ST HELENS v. WIGAN Premiership Final

16 May 1993
Old Trafford, Manchester

Attendance: 36,598
Referee: Mr Holdsworth (Kippax)

By common consent Wigan were the outstanding team in the Rugby League during a glorious period of silverware success between 1988 and 1995, as the lifting of a record number of Challenge Cups and other trophies confirms. As with other clubs, Saints felt the power of the Central Park side for, among other defeats, they nursed painful memories of Wembley reverses in 1989 and 1991, a semi-final loss at Old Trafford in 1990, plus a Premiership final thrashing on the same ground twelve months before. It was time to redress the balance and the Saints did this handsomely the following season by overcoming Wigan 17-0 in the Charity Shield showdown at Gateshead, winning 41-6 at Knowsley Road on Boxing Day and drawing 8-8 at Central Park on Good Friday, while the biggest prize was yet to come. That was an epic 10-4 Premiership final triumph at Manchester's Theatre of Dreams in 1993, with Saints thwarting Wigan's five-trophy Grand Slam hopes, and also gaining revenge for a single point Lancashire Cup final defeat and being pipped for the Championship on points difference.

A scoreless first half appeared likely until Saints' skipper Shane Cooper's chip-through ricocheted off a Wigan defender for Gary Connolly to touch down. Fully sixty minutes elapsed before Wigan levelled at 4-4, when Frano Botica engineered a try for Mike Forshaw. Wigan-born scrum-half Gus O'Donnell edged Saints in front again with successive drop-goals, and the issue remained in the melting pot until five minutes from time, when slick cross-field passing sent centre Paul Loughlin over in the left-hand corner.

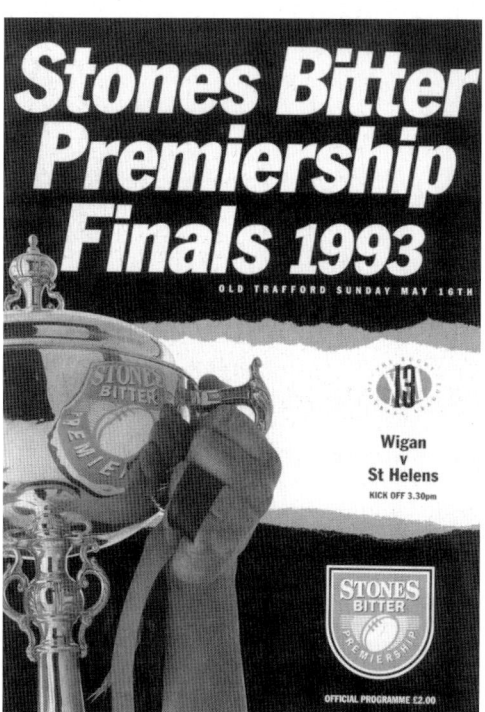

Saints' victory was their fourth in a Premiership final, while for Wigan the defeat was their first in 19 finals since they lost to Saints in the Lancashire Cup final of 1984. It also heralded the end of a run of 25 consecutive victories in knock-out competitions over the previous 18 months. A certain youngster named Chris Joynt was a landslide winner of the Harry Sunderland man of the match. There was also a special place of honour at the post-match celebrations for prop-forward colossus Kevin Ward, whose career had been tragically ended by a serious leg injury at Wigan on Good Friday.

Half time: 4-0

Harry Sunderland Trophy: C. Joynt (St Helens)

St Helens 10
Tries: Connolly, Loughlin
Drop goals: O'Donnell (2)

Wigan 4
Try: Forshaw

St Helens v. Wigan

Saints' bustling prop-cum-second-rower George Mann charges through the Wigan defence at rain-soaked Old Trafford. Wigan stand-off Frano Botica goes low in a bid to down the marauding Kiwi, but in vain. This was the climax to a day of finals at the Manchester United ground. The Academy Final was contested between Warrington and Hull, while the Second Division clash featured Featherstone Rovers against Workington Town, with Rovers' young gun Paul Newlove starring in the centre with two tries. Alas, the Premiership joined competitions like the Regal Trophy and county cups which seemingly had no place in rugby league's Summer Super League revolution – a great pity indeed.

St Helens: D. Lyon; M. Riley, G. Connolly, P. Loughlin, A. Hunte; T. Ropati, G. O'Donnell; J. Neill, B. Dwyer, G. Mann, C. Joynt, S. Nickle, S. Cooper (captain).
Subs: J. Griffiths, P. Veivers.

Wigan: P. Atcheson; J. Robinson, S. Panapa, A. Farrar, M. Offiah; F. Botica, S. Edwards (captain), N. Cowie, M. Dermott, K. Skerrett, M. Cassidy, A. Farrell, P. Clarke.
Subs: M. Forshaw, I. Gildart.

St Helens v. Bradford Northern Stones Bitter Championship

7 November 1993
Knowsley Road, St Helens

Attendance: 8,495
Referee: Mr Ollerton (Wigan)

The Saints of the early 1990s were dubbed the 'Great Entertainers' capable of producing some awesome displays of attacking football. Coach Mike McClennan, who was appointed at the start of the decade, tried desperately to combine flair with steel-like defence. When high-flying Bradford Northern came to Knowsley Road early in November 1993, they met the Saints at the peak of their powers, superbly led by the overseas contingent – New Zealanders Shane Cooper and George Mann, together with flamboyant Australian Phil Veivers. Yet it was a British combination which caught the eye – centre Paul Loughlin and his wing partner Anthony Sullivan, who ran in for four sizzling touchdowns! Saints' Joynt and Nickle, together with Northern's Fairbank and Kiwi Dave Watson had been in Great Britain-New Zealand Test action the previous day. Despite the crucial loss of their star centre Paul Newlove after Britain's 29-10 success, Bradford began at a furious pace, yet could only register a Deryck Fox drop and penalty goal for their exertions! They were ultimately forced to resort to aimless down-the-middle thrusts for the rest of the encounter, as the Saints' attacking machine went into overdrive, with a devastating 54-point scoring spree, including ten tries! It was a personal triumph for Anthony Sullivan as he revelled in the possession and space afforded to him out wide – a veritable winger's paradise!

His first try was a real gem, orchestrated by Veivers and Cooper, who brought centre Paul Loughlin storming onto the ball from deep. A well-timed pass saw Sully leave his opposite number Gerald Cordle for dead, before motioning to go on the outside. A quick swerve inside and full-back Dave Watson was left clutching thin air – a wonderful exhibition of the wingman's art. The second try saw the barnstorming George Mann use Loughlin as a foil before sending out a superb cut-out pass to Sullivan, who crossed for his first two-try haul for twelve months. The hat-trick, his first in the League for the Saints, came with another well-judged pass from Loughlin. Bradford's Tony Marchant could get nowhere near him as he streaked for the line. Try four came from arch-provider Loughlin once more, as he powered down the Popular Side, cut inside and just before he was held, popped the ball out on the inside to Sullivan in support.

The Saints were always prepared to back each other up and play the ball quickly and efficiently. Kiwi front-rower George Mann had a superb match, typified by his searing 40-metre break for O'Donnell's fine finish, and his cut-out pass for Sullivan's second. Couple this with Bernard Dwyer's burrowing score from dummy half and the magnificent all-round performance of Australian stand-off Phil Veivers and the result was never in doubt. Despite Sully's fabulous finishing, there was another marvellous piece of skill provided by skipper Shane Cooper, close to the Bradford line on the last tackle. A dummy, feint and a classy grubber put him clean through the static Northern defence for a brilliantly executed four-pointer. No defenders moved, as though time had stood still, with only Shane in motion – a truly magical moment and a fine postscript to a marvellous day's entertainment at Knowsley Road! During the man of the match interview in front of the cameras, Anthony Sullivan was just as delighted with the defensive efforts of his team-mates that kept Bradford try-less, rather than his own 16-point haul – sentiments doubtless shared by his coach. It was to be one of the few highlights for Mike McClennan and his team to savour during the campaign before his resignation several weeks later.

Half time: 18-3

St Helens 54
Tries: Sullivan (4), Cooper (2), Dwyer, Hunte, Joynt, O'Donnell
Goals: Loughlin (7)

Bradford Northern 3
Goal: Fox
Drop goal: Fox

St Helens v. Bradford Northern

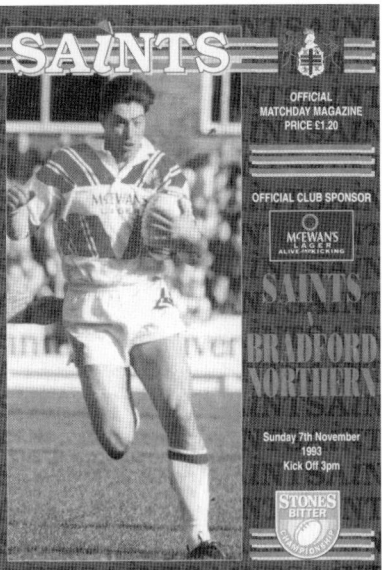

One for the forwards! Saints' hooker Bernard Dwyer crashes over the Bradford line for a splendid four-pointer, after a typical burrowing run from acting half-back. Offering congratulations is Welsh wing wizard Anthony Sullivan, who scored four scintillating touchdowns himself against the Yorkshiremen.

St Helens: D. Lyon; M. Riley, A. Hunte, P. Loughlin, A. Sullivan; P. Veivers, J. Griffiths; J. Neill, B. Dwyer, G. Mann, C. Joynt, S. Nickle, S. Cooper (*captain*).
Subs: G. O'Donnell, A. Dannatt.

Bradford Northern: D. Watson; G. Cordle, D. Shelford, T. Marchant, B. Kebbie; N. Summers, D. Fox (*captain*); A. Greenwood, T. Clark, J. Hamer, R. Powell, P. Dixon, K. Fairbank.
Subs: P. Medley, C. Winterburn.

St Helens v. Bradford Bulls Challenge Cup final

27 April 1996
Wembley Stadium, London

Attendance: 75,994
Referee: Mr S. Cummings (Widnes)

Saints brought the Silk Cut Challenge Cup back to town for the first time in twenty years after arguably the best of the 61 finals fought out at the Empire Stadium as both sides gave their all. It was a heart-stopping, incident-packed extravaganza studded with 13 tries, with every one of the 75,994 enthralled fans glued to their seats until the final hooter. It was then and only then that Saints' fanatical following knew that the cup was on its way to Knowsley Road. Post-match talking points abounded as euphoric Saints supporters headed back up the M1, but surely the one taking pride of place was a second-half comeback from the dead by their heroes.

Picture the scene: 56 minutes gone and the stampeding Bradford Bulls were leading 26-12 and threatening to trample over shell-shocked Saints in 90 degree temperatures. If there was a time for inspirational leadership and strokes of genius, this was it. Skipper Bobbie Goulding and his warriors promptly delivered in making lightning strike three times in the same place. Desperate situations call for desperate measures and within the space of seven minutes, the Saintly scenario was transformed as Goulding's towering 'bombs' into the glaring sun found Bull's full-back Nathan Graham in a tangle. It spoke volumes for Saints' kick-and-chase strategy that the net result was 18 priceless points and the regaining of the lead. This was a tactic not designed for the purist, admittedly, but given that this weakness had been pinpointed previously in the Bradford defence, one such ploy was feasible; two possible; but a third incredible – small wonder that the Knowsley Road faithful developed high blood pressure and nervous tension! Hapless Graham probably wished that he be cast away on some remote desert island after his harrowing second half on the wide open spaces of Wembley. It was a tragic irony that Nathan was outstanding earlier but, in his defence, it must be said that he suffered from lack of cover from his team-mates. First to spring to Graham's defence was Steve Prescott, who is no stranger to the loneliness of the full-back position and this gesture, along with generous applause accorded to the gallant losers – former Saints Bernard Dwyer, Paul Loughlin and Sonny Nickle in particular – by Saints supporters are typical examples of the bond that makes Rugby League the envy of the sporting world. Two-try 'Preccy' was on course for both the Lance Todd Trophy and the £10,000 prize for the first hat-trick at Wembley and might have scooped the latter award had Goulding's chip-through not rebounded from the woodwork. But there was no questioning the right of Bradford's Robbie Paul for the double accolade, for as well as a trio of touch-downs, the youngest captain at twenty also received a landslide 34 votes in the Lance Todd stakes. This was compelling viewing without doubt, both for those who made the annual pilgrimage to Wembley plus a worldwide television audience. All must have experienced the complete gamut of emotions from satisfaction on reaching the final; jubilation or despair as the unforgettable struggle unfolded; suspense as matters soared to crescendo pitch; and ecstacy or agony after 80 pulsating minutes. Given a game that lifted the spirits and a result that worked wonders in the Glass Town, it would have been invidious to ponder on contributions of individuals. It is sufficient to say that Saturday 27 April 1996 was the day that many of the lighter, younger Saints' team went to Wembley as boys and returned as men. For the statistically minded several records went by the board. Saints' 40-point tally was the

---

Half time: 12-14

Lance Todd Trophy: R. Paul (Bradford Bulls)

St Helens 40
  Tries: Prescott (2), Arnold (2), Cunningham, Booth, Pickavance, Perelini
  Goals: Goulding (4)

Bradford Bulls 32
  Tries: Paul (3), Scales, Dwyer
  Goals: Cook (6)

ST HELENS v. BRADFORD BULLS

highest by a winning side, with Bulls' 32 likewise for the losers, with the aggregate the largest as a consequence. The other winner was the game of Rugby League itself, which must have enjoyed a real feel-good factor as never before.

Defending the Tunnel End, Saints were first out of the blocks within three minutes, when Goulding targeted his first 'bomb' in the direction of Loughlin and Jonathan Scales. Hesitancy by the Bradford pair saw Danny Arnold feed Scott Gibbs and the Welsh ace powered through 'Locker's' tackle to send Prescott over, but Goulding missed the conversion attempt. Most of the opening pressure had been exerted by Saints against a Bradford squad whose Achilles heel was the failure to cope with Goulding's astute kicking game. It was from one such ploy that the fast-following Prescott swooped for his second try with 17 minutes gone. However, the one-way traffic ground to a halt when Dwyer, Paul and Loughlin sent Scales away on a 45-yard gallop to the corner for Paul Cook to land a steepling conversion. And when the Bulls' winger was on target with a penalty after Andy Leathem fouled Jon Hamer, matters were all-square at 8-8 on the half-hour.

Andy Northey limped off with a groin strain to signal the arrival of Tommy Martyn and it fell to former Bull's star Paul Newlove to break the deadlock with a barn-storming surge and Danny Arnold took over to wrong-foot the Bradford cover to plough through Nickle's tackle and restore the Saints' lead, but Goulding was once again out of luck with the goal-kick. Bradford had a massive psychological boost on the stroke of half time when, after Graham and Matt Calland had split Saints' midfield defence, the ever-alert Paul stole over from first receiver and tacked on the goal to leave a somewhat nonplused Saints trailing 14-12.

There was little slackening of tempo from the Bulls on the restart, and it fell to the man of the match contender to recharge the scoreboard by burrowing through attempted tackles by Goulding, Chris Joynt and Prescott to touch down near the uprights and leave Cook's conversation a mere formality. Distress signals were flying in the Saints camp when Paul wriggled over from dummy-half for another six-pointer and, with their team now 26-12 behind, there were premature but understandable mutterings of 'here we go again' from disenchanted Saints fans.

St Helens: S. Prescott; D. Arnold, S. Gibbs, P. Newlove, A. Sullivan; K. Hammond, R. Goulding (*captain*); A. Perelini, K. Cunningham, A. Leathem, C. Joynt, S. Booth, A. Northey.
Subs: T. Martyn, I. Pickavance, V. Matautia, A. Hunte.

Bradford Bulls: N. Graham; P. Cook, M. Calland, P. Loughlin, J. Scales; G. Bradley, R. Paul (*captain*); B. McDermott, B. Dwyer, J. Hamer, J. Donougher, S. Nickle, S. Knox.
Subs: K. Fairbank, P. Medley, J. Donohue, C. Hassan.

St Helens v. Bradford Bulls

Happily, it proved to be a case of 'ye of little faith', as Goulding launched his aerial bombardment, with Keiron Cunningham leaping like a salmon to touch down after Graham made the fatal mistake of allowing the ball to bounce. Simon Booth and Ian Pickavance then followed their hooker into orbit before coming down to earth again over the Bradford try-line. Now 30-26 to the good, Saints moved into overdrive as Gibbs and Karle Hammond carved out an opening for Arnold to notch his second try. But the 'blink and you miss something' scoring pattern continued when Paul broke on half-way to cut a huge swathe in Saints' cover before rounding Prescott to score under the posts for Cook to convert. So Saints clung to a two-point lead with five minutes remaining and it was then that Samoan Apollo Perelini latched onto a Goulding pass to rocket his way over the line for Bobbie to goal and give Saints welcome breathing space. Scales was halted by Gibbs in the nick of time as Bradford battled to the bitter end in a contest in which not one blow was struck in anger!

Yes! Winger Danny Arnold scores his first try in the 1996 Challenge Cup final, after a barnstorming break from centre Paul Newlove. Former Saints second-rower Sonny Nickle is unable to prevent the four-pointer. Ironically, Nickle would return to Knowsley Road some three years later, picking up a Grand Final and a Challenge Cup Winners medal against Bradford Bulls!

St Helens v. Bradford Bulls

Abiding images from one of the great Wembley finals! *Above:* The Little General, Bobbie Goulding, whose kicks were so important to the Saints' cause, chips over the Bradford Bulls defence. Andy Northey (left) and front-rower Andy Leathem are also in the picture. *Below:* Time to celebrate as hooker Keiron Cunningham, Paul Newlove and Karle Hammond show off the Challenge Cup to a huge nationwide audience on Grandstand. But for Bradford's Robbie Paul scoring a sensational hat-trick of tries, Hammond could well have been a major candidate for the Lance Todd Trophy. Although he did not score at Wembley, Paul Newlove finished the season as Super League's top-scorer with 38 touchdowns – a magnificent achievement!

St Helens v. London Broncos European Super League

27 July 1996
The Valley, London

Attendance: 6,286
Referee: Mr Cummings (Widnes)

This was a 'must-win' situation for Championship favourites Saints, with their deadly rivals Wigan waiting for any slip up in the final run-in. The first quarter belonged to the visitors, with some scintillating rugby. Keiron Cunningham's cut-out pass saw Joey Hayes scamper over for try number one in just four minutes, with Barwick replying with a penalty for the Londoners. Then it was Apollo Perelini – a crucial figure in the game overall – who ploughed over the line, beating no fewer than five would-be tacklers with a combination of side-step and sheer power. Skipper Goulding provided centre Paul Newlove with his 25th try of the campaign as the Saints looked to be cruising at 14-2. On the half-hour, London began to fight back, when Bawden smashed his way over after latching on to skipper Matterson's pass. Barwick's conversion reduced the deficit to six points. By half-time, the Broncos were level, after a sensational 60-metre break by left-winger Scott Roskill, despite the late intervention of Joey Hayes, who appeared to have knocked the ball out just before it was grounded. The Video Referee confirmed the validity of the touchdown, however – but it was close! A Barwick penalty gave London the lead after the break and the home side surged further ahead with a second try for Roskill, following new signing Krause's devastating touchline break and astute inside pass.

On the hour, it was the Saints' turn to reply, with a brilliant flicked pass from Pickavance to the rampaging Matautia, who smashed his way over by the posts. Goulding's conversion reduced the deficit to 22-20. Soon, the Saints were back in the ascendency, when Welsh centre Scott Gibbs stormed over from 15 metres, carrying two defenders on his back, to give his team the lead. Goulding's superb conversion looked to have killed off the Broncos – but it was far from over yet!

The Broncos counter-attacked with Tollett's pass putting Gill away on a 40-metre break. His final pass found Roselen, who stormed over. Barwick's kick hit a post and bounced over. At 28-26, things were looking bleak for the Saints. However, a couple of penalties conceded by the Broncos kept the visitors in contention. Although a Matterson swinging arm on Prescott put the Broncos' skipper on report, a kick for goal to level the scores was seemingly ignored. For Bobbie Goulding and his men, it was a 'win or bust' situation!

After 74 minutes, the Saints continued to bombard their opponents' line. Stand-off Karle Hammond drew two defenders before engineering a superb pass to Perelini about five metres out. The mighty Samoan plunged over - initially on his back - before turning the ball over his left shoulder and touching down, with momentum. In the flurry of bodies, it was down to the Video Referee – a new innovation in Rugby League from 1996 – to confirm or deny the four points. After a nervous few minutes, the try was given. Broncos' skipper Matterson was so upset by the judgement that he was promptly dispatched to the sin-bin for some choice comments to referee Cummings! Yet looking at the video of this incident, some six years later, it was no surprise to see the try given. Watching in 'real time', there was never any doubt in the minds of an estimated 2,000 plus Saints' fans anyhow! Goulding's conversion was the final act in one of the most tense and exciting encounters seen in Super League – it was a typical roller-coaster ride and a match which went a long way towards Saints' fulfilling their Championship aspirations later in the campaign.

Half time: 14-14

St Helens 32
Tries: Perelini (2), Gibbs, Hayes, Matautia, Newlove
Goals: Goulding (4)

London Broncos 28
Tries: Roskell (2), Bawden, Roselen
Goals: Barwick (6)

St Helens v. London Broncos

No problems with this touchdown! Paul Newlove scorches over for his first half try, created by Bobbie Goulding, to give the Saints a 14-2 lead. Prop Apollo Perelini's 'momentum' four-pointer late in the second half was one of the defining moments of the inaugural Super League season and kept the Saints on top of the table from deadly rivals Wigan – where they remained until the end of the campaign!

St Helens: S. Prescott; J. Hayes, S. Gibbs, P. Newlove, D. Arnold; K. Hammond, R. Goulding (*captain*); A. Perelini, K. Cunningham, A. Fogarty, C. Joynt, D. McVey, C. Morley.
Subs: V. Matautia, A. Hunte, I. Pickavance, T. Martyn.

London Broncos: T. Martin; M. Maguire, D. Krause, G. Barwick, S. Roskell; T. Tollett, K. Langer; G. Allen, T. Rea, T. Mestrov, P. Gill, S. Roselen, T. Matterson (*captain*).
Subs: R. Bawden, D. Shaw, I. Butt, L. Dynevor.

St Helens v. Salford Challenge Cup semi-final

22 March 1997
Central Park, Wigan

Attendance: 12,580
Referee: Mr Cummings (Widnes)

St Helens fully justified their overwhelming favourites tag with a stunning exposition of pace and power – especially on the flanks. Although Salford provided spirited opposition throughout, they were quite simply blown away by a classic Saints performance, including hat-tricks for both Alan Hunte and Anthony Sullivan. Despite the absence of skipper Bobbie Goulding, suspended after an incident against Wigan in the Fourth Round, the Saints could bring in rookie scrum-half Lee Briers, who slotted in like a veteran! St Helens took the lead after thirteen minutes. Loose forward Karle Hammond sold his trademark dummy and broke through a bemused Salford defence 40 metres from the line. One simple pass out wide to Hunte and that was it! Hunte got his second ten minutes later, with Hammond once again the provider. This time it was a superb pass popped up for Hunte to burst on to from 20 metres. Salford reduced the deficit with two Blakeley penalties. Yet it was Saints who increased their lead on the stroke of half time, when skipper Chris Joynt dummied and crashed over from 10 metres. Briers' conversion gave the cup holders a 14-4 advantage.

There was more to come just after the restart. From a scrum in the Saints' half, stand-off Martyn brought Newlove onto an inside pass. He shrugged two defenders off with ease, beat another two and fed Sullivan on half way. On the 40-metre mark, Sully stepped inside and turned on the accelerator. No-one could get near him – it was a superb example of balanced running at speed! Salford skipper Blakeley edged his team back into contention with his own try and conversion, but it was merely a stay of execution. Five minutes later Keiron Cunningham scored a sensational 50-metre try. Stepping off his left foot, he headed off towards the line, with defenders expecting him to pass. When he kept hold – it was too late, as he wrestled two last-ditch tacklers to the ground and strolled over the whitewash! Briers' conversion gave the Saints a 12-point lead. Then it was Tommy Martyn's turn to create havoc, with a 'double-dummy' on the left-hand side, and a superbly timed pass for Sullivan to finish off in style. The Flying Sullivan was able to complete his hat-trick shortly after, with a 'four on three' situation on the blind side, with replacement prop Ian Pickavance supplying the final pass! Briers' touchline conversion was a real gem! Resilient Salford scored tries by Rogers and McAvoy to bring the Reds up to a respectable 38-20 scoreline. It couldn't last, however, as architect-in-chief Hammond brought Hunte onto the ball from 15 metres to register his hat-trick. The Saints had the last word too, with full-back Steve Prescott controlling a long pass cleverly with his foot before touching down under the sticks. Briers' conversion brought up the half-century and St Helens marched on to the final and a second successive victory over the Bradford Bulls. Bobbie Goulding returned to play at Wembley, at the expense of Briers. Yet the youngster could be proud of his contributions during what had been a momentous Challenge Cup campaign for his home-town team!

Opposite: Saints' Thatto Heath-born hooker Keiron Cunningham amazed the near 13,000 crowd and a nation-wide television audience with a stunning 50-metre try! He dummied, stepped and showed incredible strength to shrug off the last two Salford defenders before strolling over the line. Little wonder he is so highly rated in the modern game.

Half time: 14-4

St Helens 50
Tries: Hunte (3), Sullivan (3), Joynt, Cunningham, Prescott
Goals: Briers (6), Martyn

Salford 20
Tries: Blakeley, McAvoy, Rogers
Goals: Blakeley (4)

St Helens v. Salford

St Helens: S. Prescott; D. Arnold, A. Hunte, P. Newlove, A. Sullivan; T. Martyn, L. Briers; A Perelini, K. Cunningham, J. O'Neill, C. Morley, C. Joynt (*captain*), K. Hammond.
Subs: A Northey, D. McVey, V. Matautia, I. Pickavance.

Salford: D. Rogers; F. Sini, S. Naylor, N. McAvoy, P. Coussons; S. Blakeley (*captain*), I. Watson; A. Platt, P. Edwards, C. Eccles, P. Forber, J. Cartwright, D. Hulme.
Subs: E. Faimalo, S. Martin, C. Randall, I. Watson.

St Helens v. Bradford Bulls Super League Grand Final

9 October 1999
Old Trafford, Manchester

Attendance: 50,717
Referee: Mr S. Cummings (Widnes)

True grit! How else could one describe a simply magnificent defensive display by the 17 supermen from Knowsley Road? It was the bedrock on which ultimate victory was built in a Grand Final which, given its intensity, sent a shiver down the spine. Old Trafford's 'Theatre of Dreams', and with it a record 50,717 crowd, was no place for the faint-hearted as Bulls and Saints locked horns in an eyeball-to-eyeball clash which guaranteed no one left before full time. 65 minutes elapsed before Saints mounted a smash and grab raid to snatch the equalising try by block-busting Kiwi centre Kevin Iro, which ice-cool Sean Long converted from the touchline to put Saints in the driving seat for the first time. Bradford's failure to turn pressure into points was crucial and although much was made of a disallowed try by Leon Pryce, it is pertinent to mention that Sean Hoppe, Keiron Cunningham and Iro also had touchdowns refused.

Although it was a real cliffhanger, the outcome underlined Saints' determination to honour their 'write us off at your peril' warning, following a 40-4 thrashing at Odsal a fortnight previously. There could be no doubting Saints' character and fitness levels here as they put Bradford to the sword after snatching a belated lead. No praise was too high for an incredible tackling stint by captain Chris Joynt and his men, which produced the result it deserved and worked wonders for morale both at Knowsley Road and the Glass Town.

Early indications were that Super League Leaders Bradford would have their hands full dealing with the awesome power of Apollo Perelini, Julian O'Neill, Freddie Tuilagi and Sonny Nickle up front, while the Chris Smith-Iro wing was obviously keen to make amends for below-par performances at Odsal. However, it was the Bulls who posed the first real threat via a brilliant break by Stuart Spruce who fed Tevita Vaikona, but he was scythed down by Paul Atcheson before Tommy Martyn brought off a brilliant interception to save a try as unforced handling errors continued to thwart Bradford's game plan. The war of attrition raged on unabated and it needed something special to break the deadlock, and it came from Bradford in the 19th minute when, from a scrum, Henry Paul sidestepped Atcheson on halfway and, although tackled short by the outstanding Nickle, slid between the posts and added the conversion. Enter super-sub Long to land a penalty goal after Bulls wandered off-side and, although Paul Sculthorpe and Keiron Cunningham were tireless in their probings, Saints rarely looked like finding a way through an equally water-tight Bradford defence in the opening 40 minutes. Trailing just 6-2, scoring first on the resumption was a priority for Saints, but it was Bulls who set out their stall, first when Henry Paul broke brilliantly, only to see Scott Naylor spill his pass, while Pryce and Jimmy Lowes had tries disallowed by the video referee. When Naylor was halted in full flight by Atcheson and Martyn, there was a feeling abroad that, despite the fearful battering they had withstood, Saints were poised to move in for the kill. It fell to Perelini to lay the platform with a barnstorming surge to the posts before Cunningham, Long and Acheson sent Iro over in the right-hand corner.

Only 13 minutes remained as Long's towering goal put Saints ahead, and they proved the longest in the nerve-shredded lives of anyone packed into Old Trafford, and it was at this point that teenager Paul Wellens tackled like a Trojan as David Boyle, former Saint Bernard

Half time: 2-6

Harry Sunderland Trophy Winner: H. Paul (Bradford Bulls)

St Helens 8
Try: Iro
Goals: Long (2)

Bradford Bulls 6
Try: H. Paul
Goal: H. Paul

St Helens v. Bradford Bulls

We are the champions! Celebrations begin in the Old Trafford dressing room following the Saints' magnificent victory over favourites Bradford Bulls. Chris Joynt holds the trophy for the photographers – a familiar scenario since his tenure as captain began in 1997!

Dwyer and the Paul Brothers strove to turn the tables for the stampeding Bulls. However, the 'final' straw came for Bradford when Spruce dropped Long's chip-through, and this enabled ever-alert hooker Keiron Cunningham to dive over simultaneously with the hooter. Although referee Cummings was having none of it, Saints were home and dry as worthy champions of Super League.

St Helens: P. Atcheson; C. Smith, K. Iro, P. Newlove, A. Sullivan; P. Sculthorpe, T. Martyn; A. Perelini, K. Cunningham, J. O'Neill, F. Tuilagi, S. Nickle, C. Joynt (*captain*).
Subs: S. Long, S. Hoppe, V. Matautia, P. Wellens.

Bradford Bulls: S. Spruce; T. Vaikona, S. Naylor, M. Withers, L. Pryce; H. Paul, R. Paul (*captain*); S. Fielden, J. Lowes, P. Anderson, D. Boyle, B. Dwyer, S. McNamara.
Subs: M. Forshaw, B. McDermott, P. Deacon, N. McAvoy.

St Helens v. Bradford Bulls Qualifying Play-off

22 September 2000
Knowsley Road, St Helens

Attendance: 8,864
Referee: Mr R. Smith (Castleford)

The Saints of 2000 faced Bradford Bulls on the back of a shattering 42-4 reversal at the hands of Wigan in the last league match, which guaranteed the Cherry and Whites top spot – one match away from the Grand Final. This qualifying play off was always a pulsating affair, with some incredible tackling, although there was a nervous 'edge' to the proceedings. Bulls' second-rower Peacock scored the first try after 24 minutes, while Saints fans had to wait until after the interval for a suitable response, when Sean Hoppe took a superb overhead pass from Iro to go over in the corner. Long's touchline conversion was a gem. Five minutes later, Tommy Martyn sold an outrageous dummy to Robbie Paul and waltzed over for his team's second try. At 10-4, the game was still in the balance and Bradford surged back into contention when winger Pryce caught Martyn's bomb and ran virtually the length of the field to score in the corner, which was converted by Henry Paul. Saints' insistence on running the ball failed to produce any further points. Meanwhile, Henry Paul had put Bradford in the lead in the 74th minute with a cooly-taken drop-goal. Things looked bleak with just over sixty seconds to play, when Bradford hooker James Lowes unleashed an enormous kick from his own quarter to pin the Saints back virtually on their own try-line. The Bradford defence held firm until the fourth tackle, when substitute Dwayne West, who had replaced Newlove a minute before, was dragged into touch by Vaikona. Referee Smith gave the penalty and with the visiting fans starting their countdown, Sculthorpe drove the ball in. There were two options, either a kick and chase, or try and keep the ball alive and somehow look for an opening! Cunningham picked up from acting half-back and fed Long, who ran parallel with the 20-metre line to the right and kicked to his centre Kevin Iro. The big Kiwi had to catch the ball facing his own posts, a fine piece of skill, and passed out wide to winger Steve Hall. A cut inside and Hall passed inside to Hoppe, who returned the compliment with an overhead pass. Hall handed on to Jonkers, who found Sean Long once more. He took play to the left with a lateral run. Then, a pass to West out wide on the Main Stand touchline, who picked up speed. He slipped past Smith's attempted tackle and changed pace to beat Henry Paul's desperate diving challenge. As full-back Withers closed in, he passed inside to the ever-alert Chris Joynt – the one and only Captain Fantastic – who ignored Lowes' last-ditch attempted tackle as he dived over the line with his fist raised in triumph – an unbelievable score, with minus ten seconds on the clock! 'The most dramatic moment in Super League history', gasped Sky commentator Eddie Hemmings – and who could argue with him! Sean Long promptly ran around the pitch with the St Bernard mascot's head on, as Saints' fans could hardly believe what they had just witnessed – the greatest finish in rugby league history! Will we ever see the like of that again?

Dwayne West had only been on the field for less than sixty seconds – yet his timely intervention helped to totally change the direction of Saints' season. Buoyed by their last-ditch success, the team went on to the JJB Stadium and cut Wigan to pieces, before repeating the process in the Grand Final. Funny old game, isn't it?

Half time: 0-4

St Helens 16
Tries: Hoppe, Martyn, Joynt
Goals: Long (2)

Bradford Bulls 11
Tries: Peacock, Pryce
Goal: H. Paul
Drop goal: H. Paul

St Helens v. Bradford Bulls

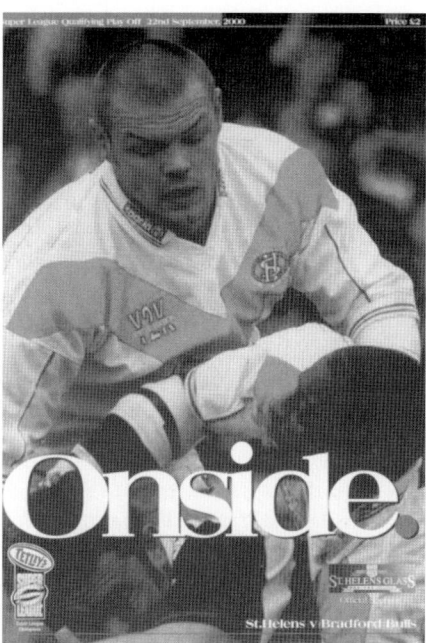

Simply amazing! Skipper Chris Joynt touches down to crown the most fantastic finish ever seen in a rugby league game. The move itself began with virtually two seconds left on the clock. The time of touchdown was minus ten seconds! This was the start of further success for the St Helens club – beginning with the Grand Final in 2000, followed by the Challenge Cup and World Club Championship trophies in 2001 – a fabulous treble!

St Helens: P. Wellens; S. Hoppe, K. Iro, P. Newlove, A. Sullivan; T. Martyn, S. Long; A. Perelini, K. Cunningham, J. O'Neill, C. Joynt (*captain*), T. Jonkers, P. Sculthorpe.
Subs: F. Tuilagi, D. West, S. Hall, J. Stankevitch.

Bradford Bulls: S. Spruce; T. Veikona, M. Withers, S. Naylor, L. Pryce; H. Paul (*captain*), P. Deacon, P. Anderson, J. Lowes, B. Mc. Dermott, J. Peacock, M. Forshaw, B. McKay.
Subs: R. Paul, N. McAvoy, H. Smith, S. Fielden.

St Helens v. Wigan Warriors Super League Grand Final

14 October 2000
Old Trafford, Manchester

Attendance: 58,132
Referee: Mr R. Smith (Castleford)

Magnificent match, pulsating performance, resounding result! These were just a sample of the joyous reasons why stupendous Saints and their fanatical fans were partying into the small hours after tasting Grand Final glory at Manchester's 'Theatre of Dreams'. An incident packed derby classic of unbearable intensity, contested before a record crowd in the deafening cauldron of Old Trafford, found five-try Saints rising to the big occasion, with defensive resolve the perfect balance to customary attacking flair. All this despite forwards Chris Joynt, Keiron Cunningham, Apollo Perelini, Freddie Tuilagi and Sonny Nickle having to break through the pain barrier to survive, in a game where Wigan fought back to within a point after trailing 17-4. This, along with Saints' stirring riposte, was pure theatre!

Having defeated Wigan four times in a season for the first time since 1970/71, Saints consigned hints of an inferiority complex to the four winds, and could rightly claim that they were now – in the northern hemisphere at least – simply the best! Every Saint was worthy of canonisation on an emotional night when Samoan cult figures Perelini and Tuilagi said their farewells, while captain Joynt earned the Harry Sunderland man of the match accolade for the second time since 1993 – against similar opposition! Four-goal man of steel Sean Long ranked high in the pecking order and, given Saints' united front, it might appear invidious to lionize others, but here goes, with new England cap Paul Wellens, Cunningham, Paul Sculthorpe, Tuilagi and teenager Tim Jonkers worthy of special mention. This story of success also reflected great credit on Saints' Coach Ian Millward, who, from the comparative obscurity of Leigh, imbued his new charges with the same uncanny winning ways that he demonstrated at Hilton Park.

Warriors exerted most of the opening pressure but, much to the delight of their massive support, it was Saints who set the scoreboard ticking in the seventh minute, when Joynt's pass out of the tackle saw Sean Hoppe plough past Jason Robinson and Brett Dallas to touch down. Long experienced his only failure with the boot, and Wigan quickly got on terms when Tony Smith's slick pass was latched onto by influential skipper Andy Farrell and he shrugged off Jonkers and Wellens on his way to the try-line. Farrell was also off-target with the goalkick, and Wigan's castle almost crumbled again when Sculthorpe chipped through for first Joynt and then Cunningham, but video referee Ray Tennant was having none of it. Having withstood a dozen successive tackles, Saints were not to be denied at the other end, with Joynt emulating Farrell's earlier effort by powering past both the Warrior's skipper and Radlinski to touch down. Long's conversion meant Saints led 10-4 with 30 minutes gone, and Sculthorpe then chipped in with a timely drop goal, while the shrewd kicking policy of Player of the Year Tommy Martyn was also helping to keep Wigan at bay.

Steve Renouf, Kris Radlinski and Terry O'Connor proved a continuous threat to Saints, however, and their line was subjected to a fierce pre-interval onslaught with both Sullivan and Wellens being called upon to defuse towering 'bombs' from Willie Peters.

Half time: 11-4

Harry Sunderland Trophy: Chris Joynt (St Helens)

St Helens 29
Tries: Joynt (2), Hoppe, Tuilagi, Jonkers
Goals: Long (4), Sculthorpe

Wigan Warriors 16
Tries: Farrell, Hodgson, Smith
Goals: Farrell (2)

St Helens v. Wigan Warriors

Hoppe in the corner! Saints' New Zealand winger Sean Hoppe scores the first try against the Old Enemy at Old Trafford. Brett Dallas makes a last ditch tackle, but to no avail. Also in the photograph: Anthony Sullivan (Saints), Jason Robinson – playing in the unaccustomed role of full-back – and Kris Radlinski.

Wellens again saved Saints' bacon with a magnificent tackle on David Hodgson in the final seconds of the half, and the next score was vital to either team's chances on the restart, but, remarkably, Wigan opted to run the ball when Joynt was penalised in front of the posts. With 50 minutes on the clock, Long evaded Denis Betts to send Joynt between the uprights, but the wounded Warriors battled back into contention with tries by Hodgson and Smith, with Farrell tacking on the conversions.

Picture the scene with a grandstand finish guaranteed: Saints 17-16 in front with ten nail-biting minutes remaining. Deliverance was at hand, however, when Tuilagi raced over from a wide pass from Martyn, with Long's touchline goal the defining moment in giving Saints a seven-point cushion. There was still time for Jonkers to hurtle across the Warriors' line for his first try in 18 months after John Stankevitch and Anthony Sullivan had made the running. Other moments to savour were of Saints' lap of honour on receiving the silverware and young substitute Scott Barrow being overcome by the sheer drama of it all. Then the party began in earnest!

St Helens: P. Wellens; S. Hall, K. Iro, S. Hoppe, A. Sullivan; T. Martyn, S. Long; A. Perelini, K. Cunningham, J. O'Neill, C. Joynt (*captain*), T. Jonkers, P. Sculthorpe.
Subs: F. Tuilagi, S. Nickle, J. Stankevitch, S. Barrow.

Wigan Warriors: J. Robinson; B. Dallas, K. Radlinski, S. Renouf, D. Hodgson; A. Smith, W. Peters; T. O'Connor, T. Newton, N. Cowie, M. Cassidy, D. Betts, A. Farrell (*captain*).
Subs: B. Malam, A. Mestrov, C. Chester, L. Gilmour.

St Helens v. Wigan Warriors

Leading by example! Skipper Chris Joynt races past Wigan centre Kris Radlinsi (above) en route to his second-half touchdown.

A family affair! Saints' players, officials and family members make it a night to remember at Old Trafford as they celebrate their team's double Grand Final success. Notice mascot St Bernard's 'Super League V Top Dogs' salute!

ST HELENS v. WIGAN WARRIORS

Celebration time for Saints' Kiwi connection as Sean Hoppe and Kevin Iro show off the trophy to the Knowsley Road faithful. Freddie Tuilagi adds the moment to his own video library!

Time for reflection for Apollo Perelini and baby Noah, who remains remarkably calm in the post-match hubbub of Old Trafford's Field of Dreams! This was Perelini's last game for the club before joining Sale Sharks Rugby Union club. He will always be remembered as one of Saints' greatest-ever forwards!

St Helens v. Brisbane Broncos World Club Challenge Match

26 January 2001
Reebok Stadium, Bolton

Attendance: 16,041
Referee: Mr Cummings (Widnes)

Rulers of the universe – and rightly so – after the unexpected overthrow of the hitherto bucking Broncos! That was magnificent Saints following an incredible fight-back in this epic World Club Challenge at Bolton's Reebok Stadium. This locking of horns by titans of the northern and southern hemispheres was an awesome confrontation which was sportingly contested apart from the odd incident. For resilient Saints it proved to be a night to remember, when passion, pride and commitment paved the way to their first victory in three attempts in the competition, with the previous season's humiliation by Melbourne Storm consigned to distant memory. Saints appeared out for the count in trailing 18-6 early in the second half but, like true champions, they bounced back off the ropes with two tries in three minutes by Sean Long and captain Chris Joynt, and then Paul Sculthorpe and Sean Long put the drop on Broncos with one-pointers. It was a triumph which gave a tremendous boost to the British game, while the message that Super Saints had finally arrived on the world stage reverberated throughout Sydney and beyond. Predictably, a massive Saints' following responded to the club's call to get behind their team and, at the same time, gave a Churchillian salute to mis-guided Super League officials who had urged Wigan and Warrington fans to support Brisbane!

Here was a triumph of team-work and, as such, hardly an occasion to single out individuals. But needs must, with the man of the match award going to Joynt, who literally ran himself into the ground. Chris was closely shaded by Sculthorpe with terrier Long snapping at his heels, while Keiron Cunningham, Paul Wellens, Sonny Nickle, Tommy Martyn and David Fairleigh were often in the picture, as were youngsters Tim Jonkers, Tony Stewart and John Stankevitch. Special citations should also go to Anthony Sullivan, Peter Shiels, Joynt and Cunningham, who were all in the wars in this white-hot battle. No tribute to the new emperors of Rugby League would be complete without paying homage to Crown Prince Ian Millward who, in less than 12 months, had transformed Saints' style and helped to win two major trophies to boot. Millward achieved an ideal blend of youth and experience in that short time and, on the evidence of the happenings at Bolton, had invested wisely in luring Fairleigh and Shiels from Australia.

Near-perfect conditions – which deteriorated later – greeted the teams with Saints sporting their once-traditional red-and-white strip. And it was the Broncos who drew first blood on seven minutes, when busy hooker Luke Priddis sent in stand-off Shaun Berrigan from short range. Michael De Vere converted. Kevin Iro, Sean Hoppe and Cunningham raised the siege for a Saints' side striving to get on terms and they may have done so if Wellens had held a difficult pass from Martyn, but the young full-back atoned with a try-saving tackle on Philip Lee. The Super League Trophy holders opened their account after 19 minutes when, after Darren Lockyer lost possession when Martyn chipped through, Vila Matautia, Joynt and Long set up a try for Sculthorpe which Long failed to convert. But the Saints' scrum-half was back on the goal standard on being obstructed by Lee and, although the block-busting Wendell Sailor was proving a handful, Saints had certainly given as good as they received in being level 6-6 on the half-hour mark. Joynt's men remained fully focused despite Sailor eventually breaking Saints' defensive line before Berrigan, Priddis

Half time: 6-12

St Helens 20
Tries: Sculthorpe, Long, Joynt
Goals: Long (3)
Drop goals: Long, Sculthorpe

Brisbane Broncos 18
Tries: Berrigan, Lee, Meyer
Goals: De Vere (3)

St Helens v. Brisbane Broncos

and Brad Meyer sent Lee between the posts for De Vere to tack on the goal. The outstanding Barrigan had a touchdown disallowed on the stroke of half-time, at which point Saints were just 12-6 in arrears.

An early second-half try from Meyer created by Berrigan was a mere bagatelle to a resolute Saints' squad in no mood to buckle and they went on to enrapture their faithful followers in scoring 14 unanswered points to claim Rugby League's ultimate accolade. For their reply was immediate when – coincidental with Millward's prayer for help from above – sleet and hail rained down as Long raced between the uprights after latching onto a peach of a pass from Joynt. The conversion was a formality for 'Longy' and with 50 minutes on the clock, the scene was set for Saints to draw level yet again when Newlove broke majestically to put Joynt over, with Long's conversion spelling an 18-18 scoreline. Brisbane skipper Gorden Tallis was lucky to escape further punishment for a late challenge as the Saints' leader touched down, and there was a hint of a famous victory for a Knowsley Road squad whose second-half performance was exemplary. Broncos' heads dropped at this dramatic turn of events before Sculthorpe and Long mounted their double drop-goal act. However, those closing heart-stopping seconds were the longest Saints' fans had endured for many a long year! Now it was time for the partying to begin in earnest, as champagne corks popped on the pitch, while beer flowed like water as pumps ran dry, with Saints' ecstatic fans celebrating the crowning of their heroes as kings of the Rugby League world!

St Helens: P. Wellens; S. Hoppe, K. Iro, P. Newlove, A. Sullivan; T. Martyn, S. Long; D. Fairleigh, K. Cunningham, S. Nickle, C. Joynt (*captain*), P. Shiels, P. Sculthorpe.
Subs: V. Matautia, T. Jonkers, A. Stewart, J. Stankevitch.

Brisbane Broncos: D. Lockyer; L. Tuqiri, S. Kelly, M. De Vere, W. Sailor; S. Berrigan, S. Prince; S. Webcke, L. Priddis, P. Civoniceva, G. Tallis (*captain*) D. Carlaw, P. Lee.
Subs: C. Walker, S. Walker, A. Harrison, B. Meyer.

St Helens v. Brisbane Broncos

The crowning glory! Skipper Chris Joynt and Paul Sculthorpe show the World Club Championship trophy to the fans at the Reebok Stadium after a magnificent comeback against the Brisbane Broncos.